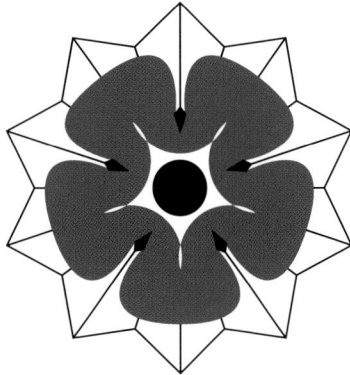

THE LEAD STATION

A DAY IN THE LIFE

CELEBRATING 20 YEARS

The Lead Station Cook Book

First edition printed 2015 in the United Kingdom

A catalogue record for this book is available from the British Library.
ISBN 978-1-5262-0003-7

Published by The Lead Station

For more copies of this book please email:
info@theleadstation.co.uk
Tel: 0161 881 5559

Designed and set by STMM
Printed in Great Britain

Dedication

To my two teams:

All The Lead Station Staff
and
My Wonderful Little Family

X

Contents

Introduction

The word 'institution' is most frequently used in any description of The Lead Station. It is famous, well... Relatively.

Since 1995, the kitchen has created delicious, simple and honest, home cooked classic food. The bar has provided a safe haven from the outside: welcoming, inviting and intoxicating - a forum for conversation and contemplation. Each day is unique, but over time, patterns emerge and rudiments replay over and over - a structure to the daily routine becomes recognisable and recordable.

Not many establishments can lay claim to reaching their 20th birthday in this industry. Such a feat deserved to be marked. But how? What about writing a cookbook to mark the milestone?

Afterall, frequently happy customers have asked how our dishes are made: the constituent parts of the Thai Chicken Sauce has always intrigued many and don't even mention the Café de Paris Butter or Shakin' what? Beef?! Seriously, who wouldn't want to know how to go about recreating the legendary Sticky Toffee Pudding?

So, here it is. Giving a little back by revealing a few secrets and offering an insight into how it has been done for all this time. Magic morsels of loveliness and mouthwatering delights, stripped back, their ingredients laid bare and the art of transformation to the plate revealed for you to try at home.

This book won't teach you to cook or turn you into a Michelin starred chef - it is not supposed to. It will however, tell you how we've done things over the years, having honed our techniques and methods through tough and sometimes bitter experience. All the recipes in the book serve 4 to 6 portions depending on appetite and are scaled down from the much bigger quantities we use in our kitchen.

We have also profiled a few characters from our world; it would have been a crying shame not to. These guys deserve celebrating, not least for delivering daily, whatever the weather, but also for the ungodly hours they keep in order to ply their trade. They are masters in their fields, knowledgeable and dedicated but rarely mentioned or known to their ultimate customers – if they are the stage hands, we thought we should pull back the curtain and let them take a bow.

And so, this is your guide through a regular Lead Station day. We've had 20 years at it, so now it is your turn.

Enjoy reading. Enjoy cooking. Enjoy drinking.

Enjoy!

The Lead Station Team

99 Beech Road
A True Chorlton Institution

The sandstone façade of 99 Beech Road has stood proudly at the heart of the Chorlton community since being built in 1885. An unmistakable part of the streetscape now, back then it was one of the new style of police stations which the Lancashire Constabulary built across South Manchester and reflecting the transformation of Chorlton from a small rural community to a suburb of the City.

But it wasn't just a place of work. Back in 1891 it was also home to Sergeant Michael Lynn of the Lancashire Constabulary who shared it with his wife, four children, two Police Constables and a saleswoman in living quarters consisting of just five rooms.

For the officers whom kept Chorlton safe in the last decades of the 19th century, theirs was a traditional style of policing involving walking the streets, taking in the occasional drunk for the night and following up on the odd missing dog.

Not that it was always easy - early in the last century the township was rocked by three murders, some sensational robberies, a few poaching crimes, one case of illegal prize fighting and frequent drunken gangs out revelling from the city centre.

When Chorlton voted to join the City in 1904 the police station came too. Thankfully the new Council never bothered to get rid of the old Lancashire coat of arms above the door and by 1925 the police station had risen in importance, with an increased number of officers and now run by its own police inspector.

But its days were numbered.

We don't know when it ceased to be a police station, but the building was certainly used as a local Air Raid precaution centre during the last world war. In the late 1950s it reopened as a local office for the City Council, the date and the stone inscription above the door the only reminisce from its former life as a police station - that and the 2ft thick walls of the old cells.

Eventually after almost a century of civic use, the building finally closed its doors and stayed empty until it began its new life as a trailblazer for all the other bars and restaurants in Chorlton.

In the summer of 1995 a kitchen was installed in the former cells, a bar put in at the front desk and the doors were reopened.

The Lead Station was born and the rest, as they say, is history.

Of course we have no way of knowing what Sergeant Lynn or his PCs would have thought about the transformation of their police station. But I imagine that they would like the idea that the building has stayed the course and is still a focus for Chorlton life a full 130 years after it first opened.

By Andrew Simpson
Local Historian and Author

The Lead Station
20 Years Condensed

Hindsight is a wonderful thing.
Foresight is amazing.

Back in 1994, the building we now know was little more than a disused office, half its current size and in need of serious renovation.

But something fired the imaginations of two young Manchester chefs.

Patrick (Paddy) Hannity and Peter (Pete) Myers were pioneering, brave and intrepid. At the time, the restaurant scene in Chorlton was non-existent - the arrival of The Lead Station was its catalyst.

Creating a simple and stylish menu of home cooked classics and comfort food, with a short wine and beer list, the team introduced South Manchester to Eggs Benedict and Thai Spiced Chicken.

In those days, there was no conservatory. Diners and drinkers sat equally scattered around wherever there was a free table, often in the garden, whatever the weather, sheltered by an open air gazebo on two sides.

The concept worked; so well in fact that more space was needed. In 2005, when Pete moved to the Cheshire countryside, now alone, Paddy bit the bullet. He closed in the garden and built a conservatory, expanding the restaurant and leaving the layout that we see today.

At the heart of The Lead Station has always been the magnificently small kitchen - the sumptuous food that has flowed out being the lifeblood of the business. With Paddy at the helm, it delivered week in and out; his loyal brigade grafting through all the ups and downs that any one service might throw at it.

And so when in 2007, after 13 years, Paddy decided to hang up his Leady chef whites and pass the keys over, he left a large void and not a little risk for his successor.

As it happens though, the beneficiary of his decision was a long-standing patron already.

Blinded by naivety and my experiences as a customer, I eagerly jumped at the opportunity. Anyway, at that time I had experienced partners to guide me - how hard could it be? And so it was that on Friday 12th Oct 2007, Alex Mauro and I stood staring up at the sandstone building that we were now responsible for and counted the number of customers file past for lunch. We lost count at 86. 'We'll be OK ' we reassured each other.

My mantra at the start was do as Paddy did - he was and still is a brilliant restaurateur. I retained all his suppliers, many of whom we still have today. I would go to market every Friday morning, looking into the prices that I had been charged with no clue what was fair, but I played along anyway.

I did everything that I thought Paddy would have but for one thing: I wisely stayed away from the kitchen. I was not going to interfere with that. I could prepare the numbers but not the hollandaise. As such, my business and future, was in their hands.

They didn't let me down. Their professionalism and resilience is something that I still marvel at every day. I wouldn't say it has always been easy, but if it was everyone would be doing it.

Throughout the years, to be part of the team has required individualism and a strong character. From the outset, the front of house team has had this in buckets. They are required to ride the waves and madness of the kitchen whilst delivering a seamless experience. Though a difficult art to master, we have benefited from the service of some seriously talented professionals; the list of alumni is extremely long and includes some fine, fun and a few crazy characters. Happily some stayed around for years creating the unique and comforting atmosphere of The Lead.

It is difficult to overstate the regard I have for my team. They have, without exception, all sweated and toiled to help establish The Lead Station as the brilliant and unique institution that it has become. An exceptional few have been here longer than me, one for the entire 20 year history. I don't know of any teams like them. The Lead Station would be nothing without them. Full respect.

Finally, any history of the business can't ignore our lovely and very loyal clientele. The team do it, but we wouldn't be here without you.

Thank you for 20 years of support.

Station to Station
Two Decades of Experience

1995 - A friend tells me that a cool bar/ restaurant has opened in the old police station on Beech Road. We soon make it our regular Friday night haunt. In Chorlton, café bars are few and far between and the process of gentrification along Beech Road has only just started. We love the relaxed atmosphere, the funky décor, the range of food and drink on offer. I ask the barman about the name. He explains that 'Station' refers to the old cop shop and 'Lead' to the material with which part of the bar is constructed. At first, the name is controversial but soon sinks happily into popular consciousness. (And could it ever really have been called anything else?...) In those early days, drinkers and diners were more or less equal in number. In '95, The Lead Station is as much bar as restaurant. Over the course of an evening, the two crowds blend and segue merrily into each other and a Chorlton institution is born.

1999 – My fortieth birthday. And where else to celebrate this mature milestone? Brothers, friends, relatives – my whole gang converge at the Lead Station where we've booked a space. One of my presents is a decorative beer glass. The friendly bar staff happily re-fill it all evening with draught San Miguel, until I have to be propped up down Beech Road. Later, back on Sandy Lane, we reflect on how fortunate we are to have this trend-setting venue on our doorstep. Diners are travelling in from all over Manchester and Beech Road is rapidly picking up.

Over the years, some bars come and go – Blue Note, Tonic, The Nose – but The Lead Station moves from strength to strength. It moves with the times. It matures with its loyal customers. Two years later, another birthday night out and I'm introduced to Lynda, a friend of a friend. She's smart and gorgeous and turns my head across the crowded front bar area. We're partners now for fifteen years. The Lead Station was our meeting place.

> **Over the course of an evening, the two crowds blend and segue merrily into each other and a Chorlton institution is born.**

2007 – Having moved to Beech Road to be nearer to its bars and cafés and closer to Brookburn Primary School (in that order), we get to know Nick and always have a chat with him on our weekly Sunday-evening dining out experience. Still offering a fantastic rendezvous point for the younger reveller, I attend the regular wine-tasting sessions and educate my taste-buds. Our young son, Ben, was always welcome from babyhood. He's been eating with us since he was born in 2003; his grandma teased him that he knew what Lead Station fish goujons were before he knew what fish fingers were! His mum and I on the other hand, welcomed the seasonal fresh menu with glee, working our way through its delights.

I used to take Ben in on an afternoon on the way home from Brookburn. His exposure to The Lead Station's cosmopolitan clientele – gay, straight, black, white, young, old – has helped make him the tolerant, worldly young man he is fast becoming. Once his nursery teacher popped in for coffee on her way home from school… and saw Ben, one of her pupils, propping up the bar just like a regular barfly! Like father like son. Always family friendly and still our favourite haunt…

2015 – Sitting in the front café area with my laptop, as I do three or four times a week, sipping my latte and working on the final draft of my novel…. A great place to work.

Free Wi-Fi and an atmosphere conducive to relaxed thought. One of my chats leads to me hearing about the plans for The Lead Station Cookbook. I offer to contribute a small piece as token of my gratitude and admiration for such a fine part of Chorlton's culinary and cultural landscapes.

And so, here it is and here am I – still a committed regular. In fact, I might pop in this afternoon for a bottle of Anchor Steam Porter. Cheers, Lead Station! We've grown up together. Here's to another twenty years….

By Steve Hales
Local resident, Author
and Lead Station regular

Mornings

Coffee Beans & the Humble Espresso

The path that coffee takes to get to your cup is very long, complex and labour intensive.

A brief summary goes like this: A bean starts life with the grower, is then picked and sent on to workers who de-hull and dry them. Coffee is then sorted according to quality ready for sale as green beans, before being carefully selected and shipped around the globe to be roasted and blended. Packed, bagged and boxed, it finally arrives with the barista who grinds and brews it for you just the way you like it.

Coffee needs to be rested for up to 10 days and allowed to release gasses trapped by the roasting process before it is at its best, but starts getting too old at around 3 weeks after roasting. It is quite a juggling act to consume it at the right moment.

At each stage of production there is an opportunity to do the job well with knowledge and passion, or to take shortcuts and accept lower standards. We only have the responsibility for the final stage of this long process, but must do justice to all the efforts that have come before ours.

There are an almost infinite number of things that affect the outcome of even a simple espresso, but only a few of these that we have any real control over.

These include:
- The amount of coffee we use
- How finely we grind it
- How hard we pack it
- How much water we use
- How hot it is
- When the machine was last used or cleaned
- How long it takes to brew
- How long ago the coffee was roasted
- How long ago it was ground
- The temperature of the cup it is being served in.

We use the mantra of '25 in 25' meaning a properly prepared espresso should yield 25ml of coffee and take 25 seconds to pour from the machine: a simple guideline to build on.

Coffee is enjoyed in many different ways – as a morning wake up for the locals, a pick-me-up at lunch, or enjoyed whilst leisurely reading the paper. As the light fades we serve our famous Espresso Martinis to aficionados and revellers alike, and of course there is still the ubiquitous after dinner coffee to serve. Whatever the time or occasion, all our coffees share a consistently good quality espresso.

Finding a blend that can do all of this is no easy task and even that doesn't guarantee the perfect brew. What really makes the difference is knowledge, passion and a little bit of attention to detail ensuring a great espresso each time. Water coming out of our coffee machine is pretty hot (93°C to be precise!) – this means that any coffee oils left behind will very quickly turn bitter and taste like burnt rubber if not gotten rid of. This is why we customarily rinse them away with a little water after every shot we make.

Then there's the actual making of the coffee itself. With all that effort going into our espresso, it gives us the perfect base for our milk drinks. The very complicated science of espresso is taught first, then the technique of properly steamed and textured milk. Eventually with practice we combine the two to create great tasting coffees with beautiful latte art, (eventually).

And so next time you're in, why not spend a few minutes watching our baristas and you will see what I mean – there is a lot to it.

By Adam Ross
Head Barista at The Lead Station
and Serious Coffee Aficionado

Footnote:
We currently grind Drury's Espresso Blend beans. They are medium to full roasted, making them dark very slightly oily.
They produce a rich and dark flavour and a versatile quality espresso. To our knowledge, they are the same beans used at Raymond Blanc's two Michelin starred Le Manior aux Quat'Saisons in Oxfordshire.

Espresso

Carefully measure 18g (or 9g for a single) of freshly ground coffee using the "overfill and level" technique or the "Stockfleths move".

Tamp hard to ensure a good extraction, then pour until just before the coffee turns bitter.

Serve with a thick golden cream on top.

Cappuccino

1 Part Espresso

3 Parts Milk
(2 Parts Milk, 1 Part Foam when settled)

Chocolate Sprinkle

Shot of Espresso from freshly ground coffee.

Silky steamed and foamed milk at just the right temperature: 65 - 70°C - when the milk is at it's sweetest.

Texture and proportion of foam most important.

Sprinkle chocolate.

Latte

1 Part Espresso

5 Parts Milk

Technically a "Latte Macchiato" as the drink is layered by pouring the Espresso on top of steamed milk.

Flat White

1 Part Espresso

3 Parts Milk

A "Short Strong Latte", not a Black Coffee with milk. The focus here is a sensory experience of silky texture, strong flavours and complex aromatics.

Serve a little cooler (60°C) to enhance the flavours. Not as much foam as a Cappuccino and a smoother texture.

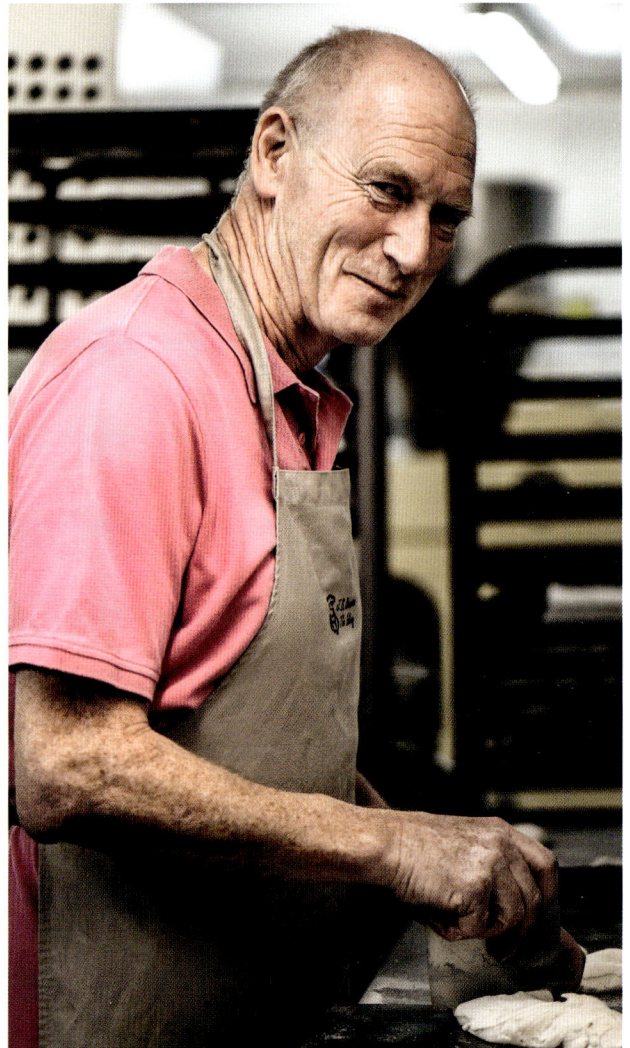

Bread & Baking

Baking bread is an art form, one that we simply don't have the time or space to master. And why would we when, luckily for us, we have some award winning bakeries literally right on our doorstep.

Peter Kellet
JB Richardson's Bakers Ltd.

Run by Colin Richardson and Peter Kellet, closest to us is the wonderful JB Richardson's. They have enticed Beech Road with wonderful smells emanating from their ovens since 1947. Led by Colin, each and every morning the team of bakers mix, knead and bake on an epic scale, occasionally producing 20,000 different pieces in one morning!

In turn, Peter serves a diverse customer base including The M.E.N. Arena and the Town Hall, feeding rock-stars and Prime Ministers alike. They have even baked for HRH The Queen and Prince Philip. And where do Manchester United get birthday cakes for the their players? Richardson's of course, having supplied Carrington and Old Trafford on match days, for years.

Peter is also somewhat of a sage on anything from fixing broken equipment to complex business issues.
"To remember you" (Pete's favourite phrase) is generally the prefix to a wise and insightful nugget of advice.

He is a lovely man, and the gentle giant of Beech Road.

Stefan Najduch
Barbakan

Barbakan is a Polish deli and bakery par excellence. A Chorlton gem, it has been operating for over 50 years and is one of Manchester's most famous food outlets.

Stefan and his team are masters of their craft, winners of numerous accolades and plaudits.

Daily they bake over 150 different breads and pastries and are set to continue for years to come – Frankie, Stefan's daughter, has recently joined the team to take the reins as Stefan slowly heads for the 19th hole.

'Front of house' is fronted by legendary 'Deli Lama', Victor Hyman; always remaining calm despite the hoards of customers. A gentleman and a scholar, he could as easily talk to you about Buddhism and karma, as cheese and ham, all in Sanskrit!

Hill's Bakers
Withington

Without Hill's our breakfasts would be very different – they supply our much admired, humble potato cakes amongst other items.

For more than 10 years this little bakery, just off the Parkway, has supplied us and we are delighted they do.
After recently changing hands, we are pleased that nothing else has altered and long may it remain so!

Breakfast at The Lead
A Chef's Perspective

8am Sunday morning Beech Road, Chorlton - calm before the storm.

Very tired after working a busy Saturday night, broken sleep after waking every couple of hours thinking it was time to get up. Ah well, got to crack on, the bartender will be in soon to make a much needed coffee. Just a few people around; early morning joggers and dog walkers. Unlock the doors, enter the kitchen with fellow chef, ovens on, extraction on, begin to set up for a busy breakfast and lunch. (Breakfast runs straight into lunch so need to get lunch ready at the same time as breakfast as there will be no time later with a full restaurant). Cook batches of bacon, sausage, black pudding, tomatoes, mushrooms and set up egg poacher and fryer. Eggs, hundreds of eggs cracked to order. Separate yolks for hollandaise, making sure it's nice and thick so it will not split in the middle of service, a breakfast chef's worst nightmare, (it can be rectified but takes valuable time in the middle of a busy service). OK, everything set up for breakfast, doors will open at 10am so need to quickly get lunch ready in the service fridges, everything has got to be to hand, can't be running around later, basically have to stand in the same place for 6 hours service. Not even time to get to the toilet, just have to sweat it out.

Any last minute prep for lunch service? Blanch chips, finish hollandaise, sear beef joints ready for the oven, start to cook Yorkshire puddings. Meat delivery arrives as we almost sold out of steaks on Saturday night, check the quality, put away and check the other meat and fish for service. Do as much as possible before the doors open - quick coffee, sort out specials with Manager and check anything that we're running low on.

10am - doors open, check Beech Road to see how busy it is, people already waiting outside - going to be a busy one. Kitchen Porter arrives to a mountain of pans. First breakfast checks start to come on, need to get them out fast to start as we mean to go on. Sub this for that, scrambled instead of fried eggs, extra this, none of that, extra bacon on a vegetarian breakfast???? Well-done eggs, hollandaise on the side… You want me to come and eat it for you???? Bigger tables start to arrive, ticket machine going into overdrive, check board starts to fill up. Floor staff asking for gluten free options, "can we do this, can we do that? Where's table 5? Did I put that check on right? - the customer wants bacon crispy, just whites - no yolks?" Please???!!! Four omelettes on at the same time and only three pans and one gas jet to cook them on, will have to improvise. Phew, relief as other chef arrives to give a much needed extra pair of hands. Restaurant's full, service bell getting hammered, get this food out asap, make room to plate up next tables. Meanwhile trying not to burn Yorkshire puddings and making sure the roast beef is nice and pink. Has breakfast nearly finished yet? 'Anyone to order manager?' yeah, you've got a 10, a couple of 6's and two 4's, oh, and six 2's. Need to get the checks in and out asap and start thinking about getting ready for lunch. The hardest part of the day is getting the last breakfast checks out while getting lunch set up. Clear away any left over breakfast stuff, another quick coffee and straight onto lunch. Relief - breakfast has finished for another day.

By Duncan Ranyard
Chef @ The Lead Station

The London Review of Breakfasts

Tuesday, August 11, 2009

It is rare that I am thrown into a situation that I am not able to foresee to some degree. Obviously, it is impossible to predict the future, but I do a pretty good job based mostly on forward planning, generalisation and stereotyping. In fact, I'm fairly flawless. Provided, therefore, with the following components - a Mancunian suburb, an English 'summer' morning, a shabby pub and an irritable temperament (hunger), I made a quick assessment: this wasn't going to be a breakfast to write home about.

We arrived at The Lead Station not so much out of choice, but out of necessity - it was the only place open that particular Sunday morning in Chorlton. We were lead through the main body of the empty pub towards the back to a bright sun-trapped garden, filled with families and gossiping friends, spread out supplements and all smiles. Tea and coffee flowed, provided by amiable staff fully prepared for free top-ups and who proved more attentive than one of those waitresses with the little aprons in Hollywood film diners. I had to do several comedy double takes. Wasn't it meant to be grim up north?

When the breakfast arrived, it was so packed with ingredients it practically fell off the plate. The sausages provided a satisfyingly crisp crunch, oozing the right amount of grease. I was delighted to see the addition of a potato cake, that Lancashire speciality...

...I sat basking in the sun pretending I was on holiday. The black pudding was so rich and my breakfast companion let me polish off her vegetarian haggis, a well-seasoned mix of lentils and pearl barley.

Happily, there was an abundance of toast and as I sat watching my little foiled slab of butter melt in the sun I felt perfectly full and content. They let us sit there for another hour without so much as a hint of an evil glare, quite happy to pour more and more coffee. I decided I'd leave my crystal ball behind next time, as my lesson had been learned.

By Grease Witherspoon

Hollandaise Sauce

Ingredients

1 Block Unsalted Butter

2 Egg Yolks

½ tsp Corn Flour

1 tbsp White Wine Vinegar

Method

Place the egg yolks, corn flour and white wine vinegar in a bowl.

Whisk together over a bain-marie until thick and creamy looking.

Clarify the butter by gently heating in a pan.

When fully melted leave to settle.

The butter should have melted through and start to separate.

Pour the butter into a jug making sure you only use the very clear looking yellow of the butter, not the cloudy bit at the bottom.

The butter should be warm, not too hot.

Slowly pour the butter onto the yolk mix whisking continuously. If the mix becomes too thick add a splash of water.

If it looks like it is splitting, the temperature may be too hot (add a splash of water).

Season.

How to Poach eggs

The whole trick to poaching an egg
successfully is to avoid dissolving the
egg in the water into a million pieces.
- this is what the vinegar is for.

First bring a pan of water to a rolling boil.
Turn down so the water is just below a
simmer.

Now add in your vinegar.
- a tablespoon

Crack each egg one at a time.
The less impact the egg makes when it
hits the water, the less likely it is to spread.

Consider the eggs poached when the whites
have hardened – after about 3 minutes.

We use stainless steel rings to separate the
eggs and keep their shape - just lift when
ready to serve retaining the perfect egg
shape.

One final tip is use the freshest egg possible
- they hold their shape best..

Eggs Benedict

Ingredients

2 Free Range Eggs

2 Rashers Bacon

1 English Breakfast Muffin

Hollandaise Sauce (P31)

Method

To a pan of boiling water add a spoonful of white wine vinegar.

Turn down to a simmer.

Drop in 2 eggs to poach.

Grill the bacon and lightly toast the muffin.

When the eggs are cooked through, take out and drain off excess water.

Place muffin on a plate.
Top with bacon, then eggs.

Pour over the Hollandaise sauce.

Eggs Lead Station

Ingredients

2 Eggs

Spinach

2 Slices Smoked Salmon

1 English Breakfast Muffin

Hollandaise Sauce (P31)

Method

Poach 2 eggs (P33)

Lightly toast the muffin and place onto a plate.

Wilt a handful of spinach and place on to the muffin.

Now put the smoked salmon on top then the eggs.

Finish with a generous amount of Hollandaise.

Eggs Florentine

2 Eggs

Spinach

1 English Breakfast Muffin

Hollandaise Sauce (P31)

Poach 2 eggs (P33)

Place toasted muffin onto a plate.

Wilt some spinach and place on muffin.

Top with poached eggs and Hollandaise sauce.

Huevos Rancheros

Ingredients

Tortilla Wraps

Refried Bean Mix

Avocado Salsa

Eggs

Fresh Coriander to Garnish

Method

Place a frying pan on the heat.

Fry 2 eggs.

Warm a tortilla wrap under the grill.

Place tortilla on a plate
- spoon on some refried beans.

Place fried eggs on top with the
avocado salsa.

Sprinkle with fresh coriander to finish.

Refried Beans

1 Diced Onion

1 Clove Garlic
- Puréed

1 - 2 De-seeded Chillies

1 Pinch Dried Chilli Flakes

1 Small Tin Borlotti Beans
- Drained (keep some liquid)

1 Small Tin Cannellini Beans
- Drained

Fry off the onion, garlic, chillies and chilli
flakes until onion is soft and golden.

Stir in the beans and some of the reserved
liquid.

Mash up and season to make a paste like
consistency.

Avocado Salsa

4 Avocados

½ Red Onion Finely Diced

500g Cherry Tomatoes Halved

¼ Bunch Fresh Coriander

2 Limes
- Juiced

1 De-seeded Chilli

Place the tomatoes in a bowl.

Add the diced onion, coriander, chillies to
the bowl.

Chop avocado and add to bowl, pour over
the juice of the limes.

Mix well and season.

Chill ready to serve.

Smoked Haddock
& Poached Duck Egg

Ingredients

110g Natural Smoked Haddock

2 Potato Cakes

2 Handfuls of Spinach

1 Duck Egg

1 Ladle of Hollandaise Sauce (P31)

Poaching Liquid
Milk

Onion

Black Peppercorns

Bay Leaf

Method

Poach smoked haddock in milk with bay leaf, small piece of onion and black peppercorns.

Lightly grill the potato cakes.

Poach the duck egg (P33)

Wilt spinach and season.

Decorate a warm plate with balsamic glaze, then place on the potato cakes.

Add the wilted spinach. Remove the haddock from the poaching liquid and place onto the spinach.

Finally place the duck egg on top of the haddock and ladle the hollandaise over the stack.

French
Toast

Ingredients

2 Slices White Sliced Bread

4 Eggs

Bacon

Method

Crack the eggs into a bowl and whisk.

Cut the crusts off the bread and place into the egg mix.

Turn the bread over making sure it is well coated and soaked in egg mix.

Heat a frying pan and when hot, place the bread in.

When golden turn over and repeat.

Serve when cooked through.

Try crispy bacon, fruit, cream or maple syrup to complete the breakfast dish.

Breakfast Pancakes

Ingredients

340g Self Raising Flour

1tsp Mixed Spice

28g Butter

250ml+ Milk

3 Eggs

140g Caster Sugar

Method

Melt the butter and milk together.

Then add the eggs and sugar.

Whisk in the flour and mixed spice.

The pancake batter should be quite thick.

Heat a flat bottom pan and when hot add a ladle of mix, gently pushing the mix outwards in a circular motion.

The mixture will start to cook and when bubbles appear gently flip the pancake over.

The mix will 'puff up' due to the eggs and self raising flour.

Cook until golden and enjoy...

My Favourite Table
Damon Gough (Badly Drawn Boy)

'I don't go out any more. I just don't have the time. I've been out of Britain so much in the last year - touring, making the soundtrack to About a Boy and recording a new album - that I haven't had a chance to go to my regular, The Lead Station, let alone anywhere else in Manchester.

My memory always fails me when it comes to remembering the names of restaurants. If I'm in the UK I spend most of my time in London and I can't think of the name of one restaurant there. The only place in Manchester I do remember is Yang Sing, the famous Chinese restaurant that burnt down a few years ago. I've been there a couple of times now and it's quite good. There is a good place on Manchester's Canal Street, a mussels bar, but I don't know the name of that... All I can remember is The Lead Station. I go there pretty much every day.

Manchester is my home. I live in Chorlton with my girlfriend Clare because its got everything we need. The Lead Station is our regular mainly because it's just around the corner. It's a bar and restaurant, converted from an old brick police station. They show and sell art (though I haven't got the space to be tempted by any of it) and there is something a little retro about the place.

Perhaps it's the tiled tables? It's certainly very beige. This sort of restaurant is quite commonplace in Manchester now, there are a lot of new places opening up. There are loads of little cafés down in Chorlton, but Clare and I prefer this place because it's child-friendly. It's usually packed with kids so we often take our two, Edie who is almost two and Oscar, who is six months.

I think the steak and chips are the best thing about it, I like the tangy pepper sauce they use (though Edie might disagree - she is a fan of their chips and ketchup). They also do some nice fishcakes and the paté is good - almost as good as the tin of Fortnum and Mason foie gras that I've had in my fridge for the past year.

I consider myself quite reserved when it comes to my taste buds. Food doesn't mean all that much to me. I don't eat enough really. My girlfriend is always saying what a small appetite I have. When it comes to food, I'd say I'm learning as I go - I'm widening my taste, especially while travelling this last year.

In LA I got into barbecue shrimp. I ate quite a lot of it. They are much firmer than the ones you get over here. But saying that, when I was in the recording studio, I would get a turkey dinner every day, for about a month. I stick to what I know really. If I cook at home I like mixing up tuna with things. But you can't really beat a fish-finger butty, with a Singles cheese slice, ketchup, mayonnaise and a bit of margarine.

When I go out, I tend to get hassled a lot, especially if I go outside Chorlton. Everybody in the area knows me, they recognise me and I know I'll never get anyone coming up at The Lead Station because it's more of a family place. It's not like a boozer. It's more the boozers where I'll get people coming up. Mind you, The Lead Station has a fine selection of all the booze you require: Jack Daniels, brandy, lagers, Bloody Marys...'

Interview by Chloe Diski
Photograph courtesy of Some Friendly PR

Lunch

Bob Amato
Amato Products, Dry Goods Supplier

If you have eaten at any restaurant in Manchester in the last 22 years, the chances are at least part of your meal was supplied to you via Bob's company; Amato Products.

He is pretty famous amongst restaurateurs and grocers. His fresh pasta is extremely famous, as is his ability to chatter.

And he is local too. Amato Products was established in 1993, just over the road in the site that is now Bar Juan, as a truly authentic Italian deli. He has been supplying us with the majority of our dry goods ever since.

Amato supply everything from specialty herbs and spices, pulses and oils to tins of imported tomatoes and sack fulls of flour, (he stocks 15 different varieties).

Amato Products longevity and omnipresence, (they have over 500 active accounts that they supply on a daily basis), is testament to the professionalism of their operation. Bob constantly reviews and updates his product lines with the best that is available and that makes him a useful guy to have on your supplier list.

He is also a thoroughly nice chap.

Soup Base

3 Large Onions

1 Head Celery

5 Leeks

Mixed Dried Herbs

2 Bulbs of Garlic

Heat up a large pan with a splash of olive oil and add the roughly chopped vegetables to this (it is a blended soup).

Cook out until vegetables soften.

Add the soup contents.

Spiced Butternut Squash & Coconut Soup

Ingredients

Soup Base (above)

2 Butternut Squash

Sprig of Rosemary

Sprig of Thyme

1 tsp Cajun Spice

1 or 2 Small Tins Coconut Milk

Vegetable Stock

Method

In a large pan sauté the soup base and Cajun spice.

Add the peeled, diced and seeded squash with thyme and rosemary.

When this is coated and cooking, add the coconut milk and cover with vegetable stock.

Cook out until soft.

Blend and pass through a sieve.

Check the consistency and season.

Apple & Parsnip
Soup

Ingredients

Soup Base (P50)

10 Apples
- Peeled, Cored and Diced

6 Parsnips
- Peeled and Diced

Bunch of Sage

Apple Juice

Vegetable Stock

Method

Sweat off the soup base in the pan adding the parsnips, sage and apples.

To this add 1 carton of apple juice and enough vegetable stock to cover plus 2 inches above.

Let the soup simmer and cook together.

When all of the vegetables are soft take off the heat.

Blitz with a stick blender or in a food processor.

Pass through a sieve.

Check the consistency and flavours.

If too thick – let down with some vegetable stock of cream.

Season and serve.

As an option, sprinkle some root vegetable crisps on top.

Roast Tomato & Pepper Soup

Ingredients

Soup Base (P50)

10 Tomatoes

3 Red Onions

3 Red Peppers

½ Bunch Rosemary

2 Bulbs Garlic

Vegetable Stock

Tomato Purée

Method

Quarter up the tomatoes and put into a deep sided oven tray.

To this add the garlic, rosemary, roughly chopped pepper and onions.

Add a splash of olive oil and place in the oven to roast.

In a pan on the top of the stove sweat off the soup base.

Add to this a squeeze tomato purée and a tin of tomatoes.

When the peppers and tomatoes are roasted and soft add to the pan.

Cover with vegetable stock, bring to boil and simmer.

Take off the heat.

Blitz and pass through a sieve.

Check consistency and season.

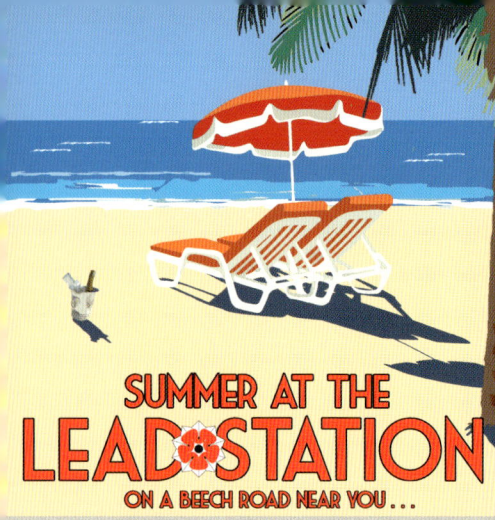

SUMMER AT THE LEAD✿STATION
ON A BEECH ROAD NEAR YOU...

WINE ✿ CLUB

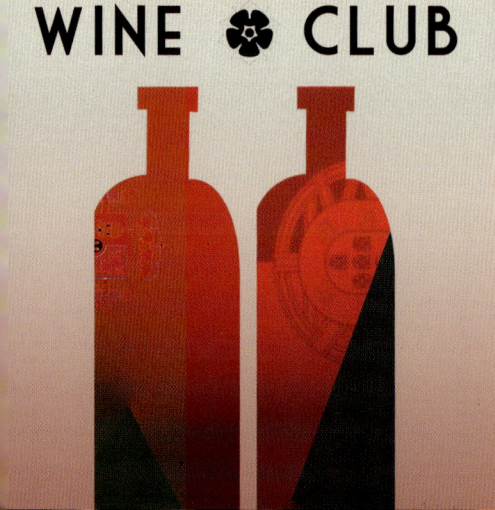

THE LEAD STATION
2014

WINE NIGHT

Ploughman's Sandwich

Ingredients

2 Slices Multi Seed Bread

Mayonnaise

Crisp Lettuce

Tomatoes

Cucumber

Mild Tasty Cheddar

LS Chutney (P73)

Piccalilli (P75)

Grapes

Apple

Method

Lightly smear mayonnaise onto the bread.

Top with crisp green lettuce, slices of tomato and cucumber.

Place two slices of mild tasty mature cheddar and top with 2nd slice of bread.

Cut diagonal and place on a board.

Accompany with LS carrot chutney and homemade piccalilli, grapes and apple. Piccalilli recipe on page P75

Pastrami & Emmental Sandwich

2 Slices Multi-Seeded Toasted Bread

Mustard Mayonnaise

Crisp Green Lettuce

Pickled Gherkins

Tomato

Pastrami

Emmental Cheese

Lightly toast the bread and smear with Dijon mayonnaise.

Place 3 - 4 slices of gherkins and sliced tomato on top.

Then add the crisp lettuce.

On the other slice place 2 slices of pastrami and 2 slices of Emmental cheese.

Place the 2 halves together.

Cut in ½ and arrange on board accompany with skinny fries.

Fish Finger Sandwich

80g coley

Ciabatta

Rocket

Tartare Sauce

Lemon Wedge

Breadcrumbs

Egg Wash

Cut the coley into strips and pane.

To pane - first coat in seasoned flour, then egg wash then breadcrumbs.

When this done place in a hot fryer and cook until golden and season or roast in the oven on a high heat.

Lightly toast the ciabatta and place on a plate.

Drizzle a little salad dressing on the bread and top with rocket.

Place the fish fingers on top, then the lid.
Accompany with tartare sauce and skinny fries.

Open Cray Fish Sandwich

Ingredients

A Slice of Multi Seeded Bread Toasted

Small Tub of Crayfish

Red Onion

Small Handful of Parsley

Lemon Zest

Olive Oil

Salt and Pepper

Little Gem Lettuce

Cherry Tomatoes

Method

Finely dice ½ a red onion and mix together with the zest of a lemon and finely chopped parsley.

Add a splash of olive oil and season.

Drain the crayfish and add to this mix, making sure that there is a balance of the ingredients.

On a plate place the toasted bread, cut diagonally, top with little gem lettuce and place a good helping of soused crayfish on top.

Garnish with cherry tomatoes and a lemon wedge.

Halloumi Wrap

3 Slices of Halloumi

1 Avocado

Lemon Juice

½ Red Chilli

Beetroot

Lettuce

Tomato

Tortilla Wrap

Finely dice ½ a de-seeded chilli and place in a dish. Add the avocado and juice of ½ a lemon. Mash this together and season.

Peel the beetroot and slice. Place into a pan and cover with water - cook until soft.

Place the tortilla wrap on a board. Spread the avocado mash down the centre, then top with beetroot and tomato.

Place the lettuce on the top.

Take the Halloumi and cook either in a hot pan, fryer or grill.

When cooked place on other items and tightly roll.

Place on a panini machine to seal.

Cut in half and serve with salad or skinny fries.

Chicken Liver Parfait

Ingredients

½ Onion Finely Diced

¼ Bulb Garlic
- Cloves Finely Chopped

15 Mushrooms
- Finely Sliced

Thyme
- a Few Sprigs

Rosemary
- 2 Sprigs

140ml combined:
Red Wine, Port and Brandy

225g Chicken Livers

225g +/- Clarified Butter
- Weight to be determined after
  liver has been blended and
  weighed

2 Medium Eggs
- 1 Whole egg plus one yolk
  per 225g of livers

Decent Pinch of Salt

1 tsp Pepper

Serve with Carrot Chutney
- see P73

Method

Sweat the onions, garlic, mushrooms, thyme and rosemary in a pan.

Add the wine, port and brandy and allow to cook on low heat until reduced - no liquid left.

This can be blended for a smooth parfait or left for a rougher look.

Sort the livers out carefully, removing any gall bladders etc. (these are greeny / black in colour)

Blend the livers in a food blender until completely smooth.

Pass through a sieve.

Weigh the strained liver purée and set aside.

Weigh the same amount of butter, melt (clarify) set aside.

In a large mixing bowl, mix the livers, the mushroom mix and the eggs together.

Gradually pour in the clarified butter whisking continuously.

Season (it has to be over seasoned at this point or it will be bland when finished).

Soak parchment paper in water, wring out, then fold in half and line a small loaf tin.

Pour the parfait mixture into the lined tin to the top.

Fold the excess paper over the top to cover.

Place the loaf tins in a bain-marie and put in the oven.

The water should cover halfway up the tins.

Set the oven at gas mark 5/6 (190˚C / 170˚C fan) for 45mins - 1 hour.

Lead Station Fish Cakes

Ingredients

4 Large Potatoes

600g Side Salmon

½ Red Onion
- finely chopped

½ White Onion
- Finely Chopped

1 Lemon
- Quartered

¼ Bunch Fresh Dill

4 Shoots Spring Onions

Splash of White Wine

Breadcrumbs

Salt and Pepper

Method

Skin and pin bone the salmon and place in a deep sided tray, with the lemons, wine, salt, pepper and some water.

Poach salmon in oven for about 20 - 25 minutes until cooked.

While this is in the oven peel potatoes and put into a pan, covering with water and allow to cook.

When cooked, strain, mash and allow to cool.

Strain the poaching liquor from salmon and put in a pan, reduce until there is only a small amount left.

When the salmon is cooled, flake into a bowl with the finely diced onions, chopped dill, chopped spring onions and cooking liquor reduction.

Add the mashed potato
(it may not take it all).

Add pepper and salt to taste.

Pat and shape into patties, then pane them first placing in flour, then egg wash and the breadcrumbs.

These are then ready to shallow or deep fry.

Lead Station Salad

Ingredients

Assorted Salad Leaves

Roasted Peeled Red Pepper

Cherry Tomatoes

Cucumber

Artichoke Hearts

Soft Boiled Egg

Croutons

Red Onions

Method

Wash, drain and spin the salad leaves and place them in a bowl.

Lightly dress with vinaigrette and arrange in a serving dish.

Arrange the other ingredients with the leaves, making sure all the different colours are visible.

Sprinkle with a few croutons.

Serving Suggestions

Grill 4 pieces of Halloumi or plain / marinated grilled chicken and add to the top

For Reni's version, lose the olives and add carrot sticks (rock it up!)

Superfood Salad

Ingredients

500g Bulghar Wheat

300g Red and White Quinoa
- Ready Cooked

500g Shelled Edamame
Soy Beans

100g Green Beans

Big Splash of Olive Oil

1 tbsp Vegetable Stock Powder

Salt and Pepper

Serving Suggestions:

Grilled Harissa Flavoured Chicken

Seared Sea Bass Fillet

Grilled Halloumi

Method

Place bulghar wheat, vegetable stock powder and olive oil in mixing bowl and mix together.

Boil enough water to cover bulghar wheat + extra 1cm of water over line of bulghar wheat, then cover with cling film and leave for about 25 min.
- This will steam and cook.

Take off cling film and allow to cool.

Top and tail the green beans then blanche in boiling water and refresh in iced water.

Cut these into 1 inch size.

In a bowl place the bulghar wheat, quinoa, soy beans and green beans.

Mix well.

Add sliced avocado with the feta cheese and beetroot sauce to complete.

Season and serve.

Falafel Salad Gluten Free

Ingredients

1.5kg Drained Tinned Chickpeas
(makes a lot!)

½ Bunch Fresh Curly Parsley
- Finely Chopped

½ Bunch Fresh Coriander
- Finely Chopped

1 Dessert Spoon Garlic Purée

4 Chilli - De-seeded
- Finely Chopped

2 tbsp Ground Coriander

3 tbsp Ground Cumin

Pinch of Bicarbonate of Soda

50ml Water

150g Gluten Free Flour

Salt and Pepper to Taste

Method

Drain the chick peas and place into the food processor.

Pulse until they just break up
- not a paste.

Mix all other ingredients together in a large bowl.

To test the consistency, shape 1 falafel and drop in fryer.

If it starts to break apart it may need more flour.

Check all the flavours are balanced.

Pat into appropriate shapes.

Shallow or deep fry.

Sides

Carrot & Ginger Chutney

Ingredients

6 Large Carrots

2cm Piece Ginger

1 - 2 Lemons

140ml White Wine Vinegar

140ml Water

1½ tbsp Ground Coriander

1 tbsp Salt

225g Sugar

85ml Honey or Syrup

Method

Grate the carrots.

Peel and grate the ginger.

Scrape the zest of the lemons, then juice.

Add the ginger, lemon zest and juice, vinegar, ground coriander, salt and water to the grated carrots and mix by hand.

Leave to marinate over night.

Cook out slowly and then add the sugar and honey.

Cook out slowly, stirring for about 25 minutes until the carrot is soft and the liquid is thick.

Piccalilli

Ingredients

½ Cauliflower
- Picked into Small Florets

4 Chillies
- De-seeded and Finely Chopped

2 Onions
- Diced

2 Green Peppers

1 Yellow Pepper

3 Carrots Finely Chopped

170g Rock Salt

700ml White Wine Vinegar

170g Caster Sugar

2 tbsp English Mustard

1 tbsp Whole Grain Mustard

1 tbsp Turmeric

1 tbsp Yellow Mustard Seeds

1 tbsp Curry Powder

1 tbsp Cumin

3-4 Heaped Spoons Corn Flour

Method

Day 1 Place all the prepared vegetables into a bowl, sprinkle with the sea salt and cover with water and leave over night.

Day 2 Drain the vegetables off and rinse.

In a pan place the spices, then add the vinegar and sugar, allow to dissolve and bring to the boil.

In a bowl add the mustards, cornflour and a cup of water and mix to a paste.

When the liquid has boiled add ½ to the paste mixing well then add back to the pan.

On the heat cook out, mixing all the time until the mixture thickens.

Add the vegetables making sure everything has a good coating and cook for 5 mins.

Take off the heat and allow to cool.

Place in sterilized jars and leave for a week before using.

Salsa

Ingredients

½ White Onion - Finely Diced

½ Red Onion - Finely Diced

½ Cucumber - De-seeded and Diced

3 Mixed Peppers - Diced

5 Cloves Peeled Garlic - Finely Diced

1 Red Chilli - De-seeded and Diced

¼ Bunch Fresh Coriander

1 Small Tin Chopped Tomatoes

1 Lime Juiced

1 tsp Ground Coriander

1 tsp Ground Cumin

1 tsp Ground Paprika

1 Lime Leaf

Salt and Pepper to Taste

Method

All vegetables should be finely diced.

Mix all vegetables and spices together.

Can add tomato juice if mix is too dry.

Season and chill.

Houmous

1.5kg Tinned Chick Peas - drained weight

1 Dessert Spoon Ground Cumin

2 Lemons Juiced

1 Dessert Spoon Tahini

1 Dessert Spoon Garlic Purée

½ tsp White Pepper

100ml +/- Olive Oil

100ml +/- Water

Salt to Taste

Place all the ingredients into a food processor or using a stick bender blitz until a smooth paste.

Check the consistency, adding more water if too thick.

Check the flavours.

You should be able to taste a hint of all the ingredients.

Serve with warm toasted pitta bread.

Tapenade

Ingredients

2 Handfuls Sun Dried Tomatoes

4 Handfuls Black Olives

4 Handfuls Capers

4 tbsp Tomato Purée

Olive Oil

Method

Soak sun-dried tomatoes in boiling water.

Place the olives and capers in the blender.

Roughly chop the sun-dried tomatoes then add to blender.

Add the tomato purée and olive oil.

Blitz until it binds together.

Paste should be quite course, not too smooth.

Tunisian Aubergine Dip

1 Large Aubergine

1 Small Tin Chopped Tomatoes

1 Onion - Finely Diced

3 Garlic Cloves

1 tsp Fresh Ginger - Grated

Pinch Ground Cumin

Pinch Ground Coriander

Pinch Ground Paprika

1 - 2 Roasted Red Peppers - Diced

Sweat spices, garlic, and onion in olive oil until softened.

Finely dice aubergine, pour over some olive oil, grill lightly and add to pan.

Add the tinned tomatoes.

Cook out.

To finish, season, add the roasted peppers, chopped coriander and spring onions.

Beetroot Dip

Ingredients

3 Large Beetroot

1 tbsp Greek Yoghurt

¼ Bunch Parsley

¼ Bunch Mint

¼ Bunch Dill

1 Dessert Spoon Garlic Purée

Pinch of Chilli Flakes

Salt and Pepper

Method

Wrap the beetroot in tin foil and bake in oven on bed of rock salt.

When beetroot is cooked through (pierce with a knife) until soft, take out of oven and allow to cool.

Peel the beetroot and roughly chop and place in a blender.

Add the Greek yoghurt, parsley, mint and dill and blitz together.

Then add garlic and chilli flakes.

Check consistency and seasoning.

Chill and serve.

Tzatziki

1 Cucumber

4 Chef Spoon Greek Yoghurt

½ Bunch Mint

1 Dessert Spoon Garlic Purée

Salt and Pepper

Cut the cucumber lengthways and de-seed with a spoon.

Grate cucumber in bowl then add table spoon of salt and place them in colander.

After 10 minutes squeeze excess water from cucumber.

Place in a bowl.

Add rest of ingredients and mix well.

Check for seasoning.

Edamame

Ingredients

500g Edamame Pea Pods
-100g a Portion

Chilli Flakes

Maldon Sea Salt

Olive Oil

Method

In a bowl place the Edamame pods, (100g per portion) add a pinch of chilli flakes, sea salt and a tea spoon of olive oil and mix together.

Place in the microwave for 20-30 sec

Stir and serve - suck out the beans from the skin to get the flavour from the chilli and sea salt.

Bocconcini

Ingredients

Small Mozzarella Pearls
- 8 Pearls per portion as a dip/ starter

Basil Pesto

2 Cloves of Garlic

Grated Parmesan

Olive Oil

Breadcrumbs

Eggwash

3 - 4 Sun Blushed Tomatoes

Method for the pesto

Blitz together a bunch of fresh basil, 2 cloves of garlic, with extra virgin olive oil. Add a table spoon of grated Parmesan cheese and season. (Toasted pine nuts can be added and blitzed into this mix)

Bocconcini

Double crumb each mozzarella pearl - first place into seasoned flour and coat (shaking off excess), Dip into egg wash and then place into seasoned breadcrumbs making sure it is all covered.
Shake off excess crumbs and put back into the egg wash, then the crumbs again.

This is now ready to cook.

Place in a deep fat fryer, for only a few minutes. When you start to see the mozzarella melt,take out, lightly season with salt and serve in a bowl.

Drizzle over some basil pesto and garnish with sun blush tomatoes.

Tomato & Basil Bruschetta

Ingredients

1 Ciabatta Sliced

4 Vine Tomatoes

½ Red Onion

8 Leaves Fresh Basil

Olive Oil

Seasoning

Method

Cross the top of the tomatoes and drop into boiling water for a few seconds.

Cool then peel the skin off.

Cut into quarters and remove the insides so you are left with the firm flesh.

Finely dice the flesh.

Peel the onion and finely dice.

Finely chop the basil and mix all the ingredients together in a bowl.

Add a splash of olive oil and season.

Brush a little garlic oil on the sliced ciabatta and bake in oven for 10 minutes until crisp.

Top the breads with the tomato mix and serve.

Garnish with balsamic glaze and rocket.

Baker Chips

Ingredients

4 Large Baking Potatoes

Method

Pierce the potatoes and bake in the oven until cooked through.

Allow to cool.

Once cold cut into wedges - half, then each half into 2 or 3 depending on the size of the potatoes.

Deep fry in hot oil until crisp.

Season and serve.

Garlic Bread

225g Butter

6 Cloves Garlic

Fresh Parsley

Ciabatta Bread

Peel the garlic and blitz with the softened butter. Add chopped parsley.

Make partial cuts into the ciabatta and fill with a generous amount of garlic butter.

Bake in the oven until butter has melted and bread has toasted, then serve.

Garlic Bread with Cheese & Tomato

Ciabatta

350g Tin Chopped Tomatoes

Tomato Purée

Fresh Chives

1 tbsp Freshly Grated Parmesan

Garlic Butter

100g Mixed Grated Cheese (Cheddar, Red Leicester and Mozzarella)

Drain the excess liquid from the tin of tomatoes by pushing through a sieve.

Add enough purée to make it a spreadable paste.

Season with salt and pepper.

Add Parmesan and chopped chives.

Cut ciabatta in half length ways and spread with garlic butter.

On top of this spread with the tomato paste, then sprinkle with cheese.

Bake in the oven until cheese has melted.

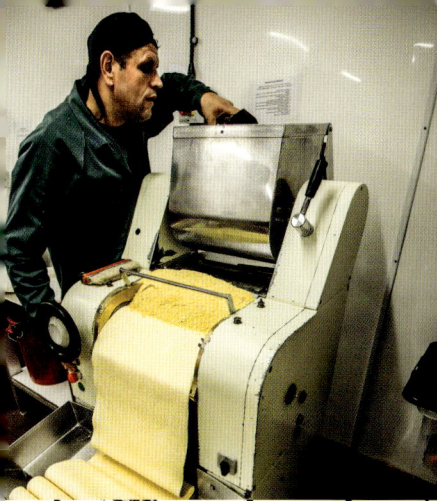

Specials

Soup: Tomato + Coriander

* Game Bangers on a bed of mash with onion rings £8·95

Ravioli: Squid ink pasta filled with crab in a cherry tomato & chilli dressing

Kids

Kids

Family friendly is a phrase that should be banned. Just friendly would be better.

With that said, customers often comment on the fact that kids love it at The Lead Station. Maybe it is the space and light inside or maybe the menu - the kids Bolognese is a firm favourite. It could even just be the fact that many have been coming since before they could walk, but whatever the reason, the place seems to appeal to the kids. Certainly it wouldn't be the same without them.

Being somewhere the whole family can come to has been extremely important to The Lead Station and a large part of its success. We also like to hear that, in some cases, we have been a large part of some families' lives too. What a privilege.

So, though this section is pretty short, they form a big part of our life and long may that continue.

Tomato Concasse

Ingredients

1 Small Onion

2 Sticks of Celery

½ Leek

Mixed Dried Herbs

1 Clove Garlic

Tomato Purée

1 Small Tin of Tomatoes

450ml Veg Stock

Method

Roughly chop the onions, celery, leek and place into a hot pan with a splash of olive oil.

Add the herbs and garlic and cook until soft.

Add ½ tin of tomato purée, a large tin of tomatoes and a pint of vegetable stock.

Cook for 20 minutes, then take off the heat.

Blitz with a hand blender, season and add a handful of freshly chopped parsley.

Suggestion
Great for pasta or a simple sauce

Pasta
75 - 100g Pasta per helping

Boil a pan of boiling water

Add pasta and cook for 10 - 12 mins

Drain and cool

or add to hot concasse sauce

Bolognese Sauce

600g Minced Beef

½ Diced Onion

1 tbsp Dried Herbs

2 tbsp Tomato Purée

350g Tin Chopped Tomatoes

500ml Beef Stock

To a hot pan add a splash of olive oil.

Sauté the finely diced onion and mixed herbs together then add the mince.

When meat is brown add the purée and cook together.

Pour in the chopped tomatoes then add enough stock to make sauce.

Allow to cook out. Season and serve with pasta.

Chicken or Fish Goujons

Ingredients

350g Tempura Batter

450ml Soda Water

80g Free Range Chicken Strips (3)

or

80g Coley Strips (3)

Salt and Pepper

Method

Place batter powder in a bowl.

Slowly pour on the soda water whisking continuously.

Batter should not be too thick.

Season.

To serve

Dip the chicken or fish into the batter and place in the fryer.

When the batter starts to colour take out and check that its cooked through.

Served with fries and beans / peas.

> "You can't possibly ask me to go without having some dinner. It's absurd. I never go without my dinner. No one ever does, except vegetarians and people like that."

Oscar Wilde,
The Importance of Being Earnest

THE LEAD STATION

Evening

Jack Wood & Sons
Butcher and Meat supplier

As fit as a butcher's dog the phrase goes; just being as fit as Jack would be good enough for most. He has more energy than most half his age and works like a Trojan.

Jack is another of our suppliers that has been in business for longer than we have (twenty four years and counting) and has worked with us for over six years. There is great value in the longevity of our relationship - Jack is who we have to thank for the Flat Iron steak, introducing it to us 5 years ago, now an absolute classic.

He also supplies a number of high profile accounts in Manchester as well as the British Olympic Team.

Placing great importance on local produce, using meat reared in the areas surrounding Greater Manchester, he also carries fantastic Welsh lamb used in our Posh Shepherd's Pie. In his unit in Failsworth he ages his meat in fridges the size of shipping containers for up to 28 days ensuring flavour and tenderness in every steak.

One tip though, never call if you are on the minutes. Like another great butcher I know, Lee Frost of WH Frost, he can talk for Britain.

Must be something in the bones.

Flat Iron Steak

Named so because it resembles an old style flat iron. It is less commonly known as the butlers steak in the UK. Our most popular and best value steak. A tender shoulder cut with very little fat. There are only a few on each animal and most are sent to be used in restaurants. They are difficult to find in supermarkets but if you ask a good local butcher they should have some. They are best cooked Rare to Medium Rare, anything over this they shrink and toughen up.

Rib Steak

Named Côte du Bouef in French restaurants and usually shared between two people. A Ribeye steak left on the bone, we get our butcher to cut ours into single portions by splitting the bone in half. Leaving them on the bone and the extra fat and marbling running through them gives a lovely buttery texture. At their best cooked medium to medium rare.

Sirloin

A classic and still very popular cut. Cut from the back of the animal, should have some marbling and a thin strip of fat along one edge. Can be cooked medium to well done but obviously better cooked rarer.

Rump Steak

A good all round steak from the rear of the animal. We serve ours with Chimichurri sauce, sweet potato fries and a spinach and avocado salad. Best cooked rare to medium rare.

Chateaubriand

A double fillet steak, very lean. Perfect for two to share and should be cooked no more than medium.
We serve ours on special occasions like Valentines Day and New Years Eve.

Beef Burger

Ingredients

190g Fresh Minced Beef

Seasoning

Method

Press the mince into a steel ring lined with cling film to create a perfectly round patty.

Remove from ring, wrap and store in the fridge to set.

Cook burger to preference in a very hot pan or griddle. Ensure it is cooked through.

Top with a slice of cheese and grill.

Toast a seeded burger bun and add lettuce and tomato.

Place burger on bun.

Extra topping includes mushroom, bacon or avocado.

Vegetarian Burger

Ingredients

½ Diced Onion

1 Grated Carrot

1 Chilli

1 tsp Garlic Purée

2 Spring Onion Shoots

Small Bunch of Fresh Coriander

1 tsp Cumin

1 tsp Ground Coriander

Breadcrumbs

1 Small Tin Cannellini Beans

1 Small Tin Borlotti Beans

Method

Finely dice the onion and chilli and mix together with the grated carrot.

Add the garlic, cumin, coriander, spring onion and fresh coriander, drained beans and season.

Mix well.

Add enough breadcrumbs to bind but not dry out.

Pat into burger shapes.

Sear in a hot pan then place in the oven until crispy on the outside and hot in the middle.

Top with cheese and serve on a lightly toasted bun with salad and fries.

Pad Thai Burger

Ingredients

190g Fresh Minced Pork

Handful of Julienne Vegetables
- Peppers, Red Onion and Leek

Crushed Peanut

Pad Thai Dressing (see below)

Garlic Mayonnaise

3 King Prawn Tails

Method

Cook pork burger and prawns through.

Toast seeded burger bun, place on plate and add garlic mayonnaise to base.

Place the burger and prawns on top, drizzle on Pad Thai dressing.

Add julienne vegetables, crushed peanuts, then the bun lid.

Served with extra dip and fries.

Pad Thai Dressing

¼ cup Vegetable Stock

2 tbsp Ketchup

1 tbsp Fish Sauce

2 tbsp Soy Sauce

2 tbsp Rice Wine

2 tbsp Brown Sugar

1 tbsp Sesame Oil

2 Finely Diced Chillies

1 tbsp Garlic Purée

1 Lime Juice and Zest

Add together in pan and reduce by half.

Allow to cool.

Twice Cooked Fat Chips

Ingredients

Maris Piper Potatoes

Method

Peel potatoes, cut into fat chips then blanche at 140°C in the fryer until cooked with no colour.

Allow to cool on a tray.

When portion needed they are refried at 190°C until golden.

Polenta Chips

500g polenta

2 ltrs Water

2 Diced Chilli

1 tbsp Cajun Spice

1 tbsp Vegetable Stock Powder

Salt and Pepper

Bring water to the boil and add chilli, spice, stock powder and seasoning.

Slowly pour in the polenta whisking continuously.

Cook the mix out properly
- it will start to thicken.

Line a tray with silicon paper and spread the mix onto it.

Smooth out top and allow to cool.

Cut into desired chip size.

Fry and serve.

Sweet Potato Fries

Sweet Potato

Sweet potato fries
- These are washed then cut into fries.

Blanched at 150°C, cooled then cooked to order at 190°C.

Beetroot Risotto

Ingredients

500g Arborio Rice

½ Finely Diced White Onion

1 tbsp Fresh Thyme

1 tsp Crushed Garlic

450ml Vegetable Stock

6 Medium Beetroot

Goats Cheese

Method

Peel the beetroot and cut into halves, cover with vegetable stock and cook through.

Save the liquor.

Purée ½ the beetroot and finely dice the rest. Leave to one side.

In a hot pan sauté the onion, garlic and thyme together.

Add the rice and stir.

Pour in half of the beetroot/veg stock and stir on a gentle heat.

Keep adding liquid until the rice is cooked through, then add the purée.

Season.

To serve, sprinkle with cubed beetroot and add a slice of grilled goats cheese on top.

Crab & Prawn Spring Rolls

Ingredients

250g White Crab Meat

1 Lime Zest and Juice

½ Bunch Spring Onions

1 tbsp Coriander
- Freshly Chopped

1cm Grated Fresh Ginger

½ Chilli
- De-seeded and Chopped

1 Clove Garlic

250g King Prawns
- Cooked and Chopped

Spring Roll Pastry

Salt and Pepper

Method

Check the crab meat has no shell in it and place into a bowl.

Add the prawns, zest and juice of lime.

Chop herbs, garlic, chilli and grated ginger then add to mix.

Season.

Place spring roll pastry sheet onto a board as a diamond.

Egg wash around the edges.

Add a spoonful of mix 1 inch from the point, then fold corner over.

Egg wash the sides then fold in.

Egg wash remaining dry parts and roll making sure all edges are stuck down.

Cook in the fryer until golden brown.

Plate
Small dressed salad garnish.

Small pot of Vietnamese dipping sauce.

2 spring rolls per portion.

Vietnamese Dipping Sauce

1 tbsp Chopped Garlic

2 tbsp Sugar

1 tsp Dried Red Chilli Flakes

3 tbsp Fish Sauce

3 tbsp Water

2 tbsp Squeezed Lime Juice

Mix the garlic, sugar and chilli in a bowl.

Stir in the fish sauce, water and lime juice, stirring well to dissolve the sugar.

Put in dipping pots and serve.

Refrigerate for up to 1 week.

Tiger Prawns

Ingredients

3 Tiger Prawns
- Washed

1 ½ Slices Sour Dough Bread
- Toasted

125g Unsalted Butter

2 Finely Diced Red Chilli

1 Lemon
- Zested

1 Clove Garlic
- Puréed

1 tsp Chopped Dill

1 tsp Chopped Parsley

1 tsp Spring Onion

Method

Butter
Soften the butter then mix zest, herbs and chillies.

On silicon paper roll the chilli butter into a log and chill.

In a hot frying pan add a splash of oil and prawns.

Cook on both sides until colour changes.

Add a slice of chilli butter and sauté.

Plate
Toast the sour dough and arrange on plate.

Place a prawn on each and pour the butter over.

Garnish with chopped herbs.

Shaking Beef

Ingredients

500g Sirloin

3 Chef Spoons Fish Sauce

2 Chef Spoons Light Soy Sauce

1½ Chef Spoons Brown Sugar

1 Chef Spoon Chopped Garlic

½ Chef Spoon Black Pepper

Method

Place all the ingredients into a bowl and mix.

Cut the sirloin into thin strips and place in the marinade and chill for at least 6 hours.

Place the sirloin In a hot frying pan and shake!

When cooked, sprinkle with chilli flakes and coriander then serve.

Lamb Koftas

Ingredients

500g Minced Lamb

½ Finely Diced Onion

2 Chilli

1 tsp Paprika

½ tsp Chilli Flakes

½ tsp Cumin

½ tsp Coriander

1 tsp Garlic Purée

½ Bunch Fresh Coriander

Method

Mix all ingredients together thoroughly.

Test a small amount by cooking it to check flavours and seasoning.

Serving Suggestions

Make into small patties or sausage shapes and place a skewer through the middle.

Cook in a pan or bake.

Arrange a salad garnish with red onion mixed with sumac spice onto a plate.

Warmed flat bread and tzatziki to accompany it.

Goat Cheese
& Onion Filo Parcel

Ingredients

2 Red Onions

50g Sugar

100ml Balsamic Vinegar

10ml Balsamic Glaze

Goats Cheese Slice

Filo Pastry

Butter

Spinach and Rocket

Cherry Tomatoes

Method

Finely slice the onion and sauté in a pan until golden.

Add the sauté and vinegar and cook down.

Finish with the balsamic glaze and allow to cool.

Mix should be moist with no runny liquid.

Parcel
Melt 25g butter.

Place the filo pastry on a board. Take a single sheet and with a pastry brush paint with butter.

Then Fold the filo pastry sheet in half.

In the centre put the goats cheese slice and a spoon full of confit.

Gather up the corners of the filo pasty over the top of the goats cheese and twist.

This should look like a parcel.

Paint with butter around the outside.

Place on silicon paper and bake for 10 mins approx.

Until golden brown.

Plate
In the middle of a plate place a small handful of washed spinach and watercress.

Dress with salad dressing and arrange some cherry tomato halves for colour.

Serve the parcel on top of salad.

David Levings
The Easy Fish Co. - Fishmonger

If there were an aristocracy of fishmongers in Manchester, The Levings Family would be in the upper echelons. David's independent family run business has 120 years' experience; fish is in their blood. The family established amongst others, the Inshore Fisheries shop that served Chorlton and beyond for many years and still operates as 'Out of the Blue'.

Fourth generation fishmongers, their roots go back to the original Smithfield Market in the Northern Quarter in the city centre. True to tradition, each morning their fish is still hand-picked from New Smithfield Market, or sourced directly from a trusted network of coastal suppliers, ensuring the freshness and quality we demand.

David runs The Easy Fish Co. with his son Charlie and supplies The Lead Station from their shop in Heaton Moor. Not content with just being a quality fishmonger, the shop doubles as a fabulous fish restaurant from Wednesdays to Saturdays.

It is well worth a visit!

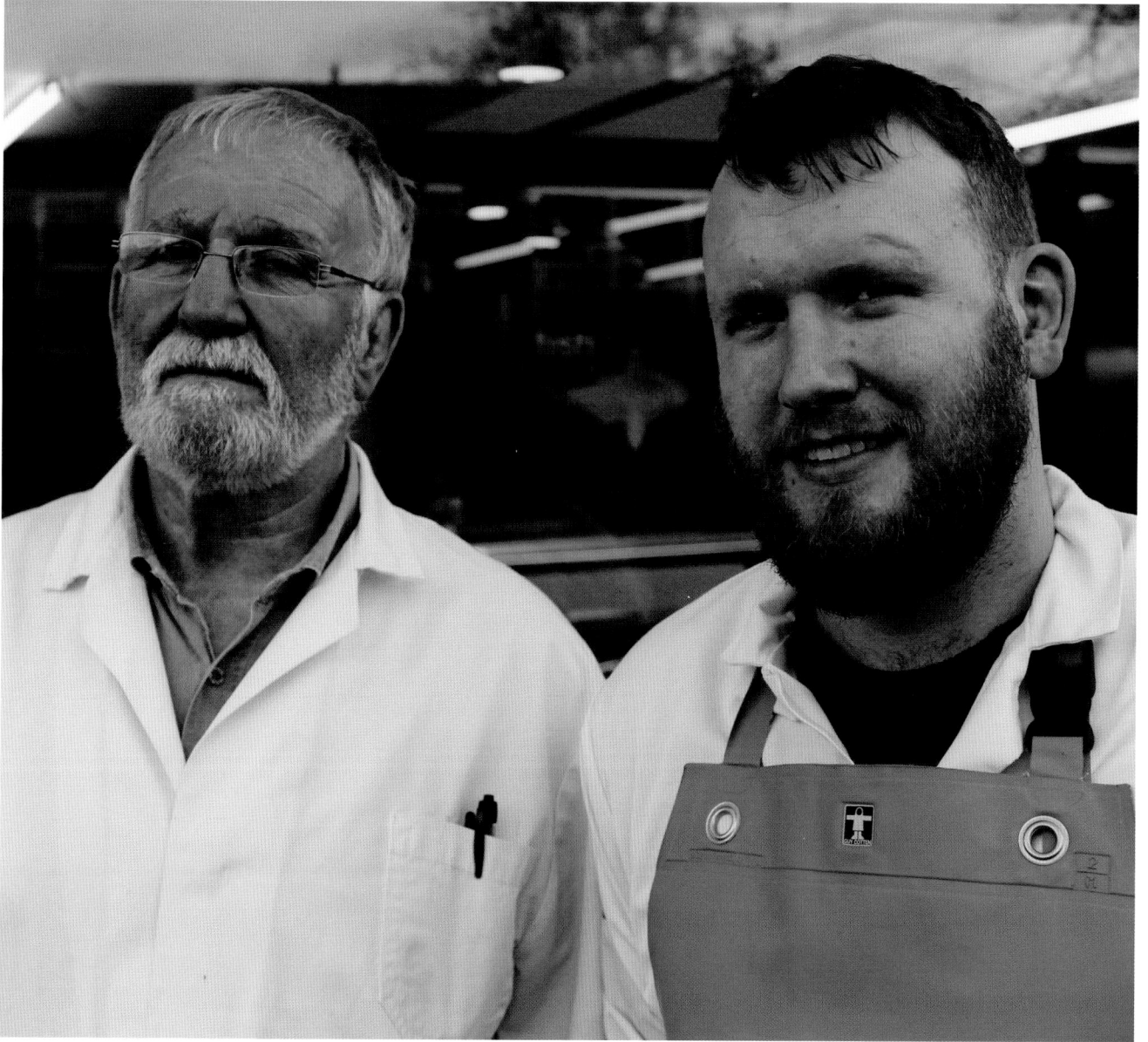

Mussels Base &
Moules Mariniere

Ingredients

2 Onions
- Diced

1 Leek
- Diced

Garlic Butter

Lemon Wedge

Glass White Wine

Small Carton Double Cream
(for Mariniere)

Method

Clean mussels, making sure the beards are pulled off and no obvious barnacles are left.

The mussels should be closed. If they are open, tap to close. If they do nothing, throw away as they are dead.

Rinse with cold water.

Heat up a frying pan, add a knob of garlic butter and a handful of base mix.

Sauté, then place a soup bowl of mussels in the pan.

Add a splash of white wine and a lemon wedge.

Allow mussels to steam open.

For Mariniere - add a splash of cream and reduce to a nice thick sauce.

Place mussels in a serving dish.

Taste, season
– add more garlic if required.

Serve and sprinkle with parsley.

This portion is a starter for 1 person.

Use a larger pan for more than one.

Pancetta, Apple & Cider Mussels

Ingredients

Mussel Base
- 300g for a starter or 500g for main

Pancetta

Apples

Apple Cider

Crème Fraiche

Method

Heat up a frying pan with a knob of garlic butter and add the diced Pancetta.

Sauté until crisp, then add the Mussel base and mussels.

Add the diced apple and cider and allow to steam open.

Finish with a large spoon of crème fraiche, parsley and seasoning.

Serve.

Warm crusty bread or skinny fries go well.

Thai Spiced Mussels

Ingredients

Mussel Base
- 300g for a starter or 500g for main

Thai Paste (P154)

White Wine

Coconut Milk or Cream

Chopped Coriander

Method

Heat up the frying pan with a knob of butter, the Thai paste and handful of Mussel base.

Add the mussels and white wine
– allow to steam open.

Either add some coconut milk or cream and bring to boil.

Sprinkle with coriander, season and serve.

Tomato, Red Wine
& Chorizo Mussels

Ingredients

Mussel Base
- 300g for a starter or 500g for main

Garlic Butter

Red Wine

Chorizo

Concasse Sauce (P90) or
Fresh Cherry Tomatoes Halved

Spring Onion

Method

Heat pan with a little butter; add the
Chorizo and the mussel base – sauté.

Add the mussels and red wine to steam
open.

Add the cherry tomatoes and spring onion,
season and serve.

or

Add a couple of ladles of Concasse
sauce or passata.

Season and serve.

Seabass & Scallops

Ingredients

Minted Edamame and Pea Purée
500g Edamame Peas

250g Garden Peas

20 Mint Leaves

1 Juiced Lime

3 Dessert Spoons Grated Parmesan

Salt and Pepper

Seabass
1 Fillet Per Portion

Scallops
3 Per Portion

New Potatoes
3 Per Portion Halved

Micro Herbs or Pea Shoots
to Garnish

Method

Place all of the ingredients into a bowl and using a stick blender, blitz together.
Add some water to help with this.
Should be thick and spreadable.

Check the flavours – that you can taste the mint etc.

Place new potatoes into a pan of boiling water and cook until soft, then cut in half.

In a hot pan add a little olive oil then place in the seasoned seabass, skin side down

Let the skin crisp up before turning it over and add the scallops.

After a few minutes turn the scallops.

Season.

On a warm plate, place a spoonful of pea purée and smear.

Place the new potato halves in a line, then place the sea bass fillet on top.

Arrange the scallops on the plate.

Garnish with a sprinkle of micro herbs or pea shoots and lemon wedge.

Lead Station Fish Pie

Ingredients

100g Salmon

100g Coley

1 Bunch Dill

1 Bag of Frozen Spinach

Mashed Potato

Roux / Sauce
250g Butter

250g Flour

1 ltr Milk

Splash of Cream

Fish Stock
Fish Bones

Water / Milk

Onion, Leek, Celery,
Bay Leaf, Lemon

Method

Place the fish bones in a pan with the veg and lemon and cover with ½ water and ½ milk.

Bring to the boil then simmer for 20 mins.

Strain and pass through a sieve.

In a pan place the butter to melt, then add the flour and cook out.

Add the fish stock a little at a time and mix thoroughly before adding more stock, keep up the process until you have a thick, smooth sauce.

Finish with a splash of cream and season.

Defrost a bag of spinach. Wring out the excess water then chop.

Sauté off very finely diced onion then add to the spinach blend with a splash of fish sauce until smooth - season.

Cube the fish of in a bowl and add some chopped dill and enough sauce to bind.

In a ring – layer the fish, then spinach and finally top with mashed potato.

Bake in the oven for 20 - 25 mins.

Serve with steamed greens and extra sauce.

Goan Fish Curry

Ingredients

1 tsp Mustard Seeds

150g Skin on Cod Fillet Portion

3 King Prawn Tails

Spinach

1 Small Onion

1 Cinnamon Stick

10g Piece Ginger

7 Cloves Garlic

1 - 3 Chillies

1 tsp Ground Cumin

2 tsp Ground Coriander

½ tsp Turmeric

½ tsp Garam Masala

2 tsp Tomato Purée

2 Tins Coconut Milk

1 Small Tin Chopped Tomatoes

250ml to 500ml Vegetable Stock

Method (Goan Sauce)

Heat a pan and roast the mustard seeds. Once they start popping turn heat down and add the onions and cinnamon.

Cook out until golden and soft.

In a food processor blend ginger, garlic, chillies, then add this to the pan with the spices.

Cook out then add the tomato purée, coconut milk and tinned tomatoes.

If too thick add some vegetable stock.

Cook out, stirring occasionally.

Check consistency and seasoning.

Method (Curry)

Place the seasoned cod, skin side down into a hot pan and let the skin crisp up.

Transfer into an oven proof dish adding 3-4 prawn tails and a ladle full of Goan Sauce.

Bake for 10-15 minutes.

Place 2 handfuls of spinach, a knob of butter and seasoning into a dish, cover and microwave for 10 seconds.

On a warm dish arrange the food. Place the sauce, the cod, prawns then the spinach.

Accompany with rice sprinkled with fresh coriander.

Fish & Chips

Ingredients

Batter
250g Plain Flour

1 tsp Turmeric

400ml Lager

Salt and Pepper

Mushy Peas
1kg Green Split Peas

2lts Water (+/- 500ml)

1 tsp Bicarbonate of Soda

Salt and Pepper

Method

Batter
Whisk all the ingredients together making sure there are no lumps.

Batter should be loose and not too thick.

Mushy Peas
Soak the peas in water for an hour and drain.

Place the peas, water and bi-carb in a pan and simmer.

Skim the top as and when and allow to cook out and mush.

Season.

To Serve
Season the fish fillet (haddock/cod etc.) and place into the batter.

Lift and shake off any excess batter before placing into the fryer.

Turn the fish over making sure you get an even colour on both sides.

When the fish is golden brown take out and place on paper towels. Season with salt.

On a warm plate place a quenelle of mushy peas, desired chip accompaniment and place the fish on top.

Garnish with a lemon wedge and tartare sauce.

Claridges Chicken Pie

Ingredients

Free Range Chicken Breast
- Diced

Pearl Onion
- Peeled and Blanched

Button Mushrooms
- Washed

Pancetta
- Diced

Tarragon
- Chopped

Sherry

Double Cream

Chicken Stock

Filo / Puff Pastry

Method

In a hot pan sauté the diced Pancetta, then add the chicken, onion, mushrooms and fresh tarragon and chicken stock to cover.

Cook out on a slow heat.

When cooked, drain liquid and return to the pan.

Add a cup of sherry and reduce by half. Then add same amount of double cream and reduce until a thicker consistency.

Check flavour and seasoning.

Allow to cool.

Add the filling back to the sauce.

Place in a deep dish and cover with 2 layers of filo pastry or puff pastry.

Bake until pastry is cooked through, crispy and golden brown.

Bangers & Mash

Ingredients

Mash
4 Large Potatoes

25g Butter

200/250ml Double Cream

Salt and Pepper

Bangers
12 Sausages

1 Large Onion

Batter
- See Fish and Chips (P133)

Onion Confit
- See Starter Goats Cheese in Filo
  on P119

Method

Peel and dice the potatoes.

Place into a pan and cover with cold water and bring to boil.

When the potatoes are cooked though drain into a colander.

Rice the potatoes (or mash) in a bowl, adding the butter and the cream.
(May need more or less depending on how dry the potatoes are).

Prick the sausages and place in the oven to cook until golden.

Slice the onion into rings.
- Not too thin (up to 1cm thick)

Dip the onion rings in the beer batter, shake off excess batter and place into the fryer.

Turn the rings over to get an even colour.

On warm plates, quenelle the mash. Place 3 sausages on top, a spoonful of onion confit, then the onion rings.

Serve with gravy.

Posh Shepherd's Pie

Ingredients

1 Lamb Shoulder
- Boned and Rolled

2 Carrots

1 Onion

Rosemary and Mint

10 Carrots

100g Butter

6 Large Potatoes

150ml Cream

50ml Truffle Oil

25g Butter

Method

In a dip dish place the carrot and onion to act as a trivet.

Season the lamb and place on top along with the rosemary and mint.

Add a pint or 2 of water and cover with foil and put into a moderate heated oven (180°C / 160°C fan) for approx 3 hours - until the meat falls apart.

Strain the liquid from the meat pan and reduce to a rich liquor.

Pull the meat apart (shred) then add the liquor to this.

Boil the carrots and once cooked, drain then mash with butter. Add salt and pepper.

Peel the potatoes, cube then place in a pan.

Bring to the boil then simmer until cooked.

Drain and rice them.

Add the butter, some cream and truffle oil then mix until fluffy.

Season.

In a large ring construct the pie.

½ meat, ¼ carrot purée and ¼ - ½ mash.
Bake in the oven for approx 25 minutes or until piping hot.

Serve with steamed greens and gravy.

Lamb Hot Pot

Ingredients

2kg Diced Leg Lamb

4 Onions
- Finely Diced

3 tbsp Rosemary

2 Chef Spoons Garlic Purée

Meat Stock

1 Block Butter

10 Carrots
- Thinly Sliced

6 Leeks
- Thinly Sliced

20 + New Potatoes
- Boiled, Cooled and Sliced

Method

In a very hot, thick bottomed oven proof pot, seal off the lamb and colour.

Once sealed, add the onion to the pot and deglaze by splashing in red wine.

Add the herbs and garlic then cover with meat stock.

Cover and place in the oven to slow cook until tender.

When cooked drain the excess liquid and reduce until thickened.

Add back to meat. Check seasoning.

Melt the butter in a pan and add the carrot and leeks.

Cook out until soft and glazed.

Check seasoning.

In an oven proof dish place a generous amount of meat and gravy at the bottom.

Top with a layer of mixed carrot and leek, then arrange the sliced potatoes on top.

Cook in the oven for 20-30 mins until the potatoes are hot and crisp.

Serve with crusty bread and red pickled cabbage.

Chicken Supreme

Ingredients

4 Chicken Breasts

4 Large Potatoes

¼ Savoy Cabbage Shredded

6 Rashers Bacon

200g Fine Beans

4 - 6 Slices Prosciutto Ham

1 Large Squash

Method

Bubble and Squeak
Peel and cook the potatoes, then drain and rice or mash.

Grill the bacon and slice.

Slice the cabbage and cook.

Add all 3 ingredients together and season.

Shape into patties.

Squash Purée
Peel the butternut squash, de-seed and cube.

Place in a pan and cover with water.

Cook until soft then drain.

Mash with a small amount of butter and season.

Wrapped beans
Blanch the green beans in boiling water and refresh.

Place a slice of prosciutto on a board, add 8 - 10 beans and roll.

In a hot pan place the chicken, skin side down and seal, turning over when golden. Place in the oven to finish cooking 15 - 20 minutes.

Seal the wrapped beans and Bubble and Squeak patties in the same pan and transfer to the oven.

Heat the squash purée and arrange on the plate with the other ingredients,

Slice chicken and serve.

Harry Walker
Cheshire Wholesale Fruit & Veg

Wise cracking and fast-talking with the worst writing in Manchester, Harry keeps very strange hours.

He wakes at 3 or 4pm and normally starts work at around 1am.
(Any post work drink happens at 11am, fine wine being his tipple.)

Luckily for us he does, as having a great fruit and vegetable supplier is a must. He has supplied The Lead Station for 20 years and is a New Smithfield Market stalwart.

Mushroom Rosti Stack

Ingredients

2 - 3 Large Potatoes
- Grated

2 Carrots
- Grated

1 Large Onion
- thinly sliced

1 Egg

2 Dessert Spoons Chopped Herbs

Salt and Pepper

Filling
1kg Mushrooms / Spinach

25g / 50g Garlic Butter

200ml / 300ml Double Cream

Method

Place the grated potatoes, carrots and sliced onion into a bowl.

Add 1 whisked egg, herbs and salt and pepper.

Place a sheet of silicone paper into a baking tray.

Gather a handful of mix and squeeze off excess liquid. Place onto the tray in desired shape, usually round.

Press down and flatten.
Continue until you have used all the mix.

Place into the oven gas mark 6
(200°C or 180°C fan) for approx 20 - 25 mins.

When cooked they should be firm and crisp.

Place garlic butter (25g) into a hot pan,, adding the sliced mushrooms and sauté.

Add the cream and allow to bubble and thicken - spinach can also be added.

Season and serve.

Place a rosti in a ring on a warm plate with a final rosti to top

Remove the ring
- add more sauce if needed.

Garnish with pesto and serve.

Harissa Roast Vegetables
with Halloumi

Ingredients

5 Red Onions

2 Onions

1 Red Pepper

1 Green Pepper

1 Yellow Pepper

2 Courgettes

Mixed Dried Herbs

Garlic Purée

2 Halloumi

Harissa Paste

Splash of Olive Oil

Method

Peel the onions, cut into half then each half into thirds.

De-seed all peppers and roughly cut into 2 cm pieces.

Cut the courgettes ½ length ways and then into chunks.

Mix together with a chef spoon of garlic and handful of mixed herbs.

Add a splash of olive oil and roast in the oven until softened.

Unwrap the Halloumi and cut each block into 12 cubes, then coat with Harissa paste.

In a frying pan sauté the marinated Halloumi, then add the roast vegetables.

Season with salt and pepper.

Serve in a bowl with a dollop of Tzatziki and warm toasted pitta bread.

Extra Harissa paste optional.

Crispy
Sweet Potato Cakes

Ingredients

1 Large Onion

2 Red Chillies

1 Lemon Zest

1 tsp Garlic Purée

1 Level tsp Spanish Paprika

3 Large Sweet Potatoes

250g Frozen Spinach

1 - 2 Handfuls of Breadcrumbs

Method

Peel and cube the sweet potatoes then place into a pan.
Cover with hot water then boil.

Take off heat when soft and drain.

Place a medium pan on the heat with a splash of olive oil.

Add the onion, garlic and chilli and sauté until soft, then add the paprika and spinach.

Cook out until spinach is cooked through and take off heat.

Place mix into a large bowl and add the cooked sweet potato mixing well.

Add the lemon zest and seasoning.

Add enough breadcrumbs to bind the mix so it can be made into burger shapes.

The mix should be soft but not gooey.

Pat into burger shapes.

Sear in a pan to crisp the outside, then bake for 10 to 15 minutes.

Spicy
Ratatouille

Ingredients

2 Courgettes

1 Red Pepper

1 Green Pepper

1 Yellow Pepper

1 - 2 Red Onions

1 - 2 Cloves Garlic

1 - 2 Red Chillies

Pinch Dried Mixed Herbs

2 tbsp Tomato Paste

Splash Sweet Chilli Sauce

Method

De-seed peppers and cut into a large dice with the onions and courgettes.

Place in a hot pan with a splash of olive oil and cook out.

Add the garlic, chillies and mixed herbs.

When vegetables start to soften add the tomato paste and sweet chilli sauce.

Stir well and cook for another 10 minutes.

Check the seasoning and add salt and pepper if required.

Au Poivre Sauce

Ingredients

450g Sliced Mushrooms

1 tbsp Cracked Black Pepper

100ml Red Wine

Shot Brandy

200ml Beef Stock

300ml Double Cream

Method

Heat pan, adding small amount of oil.

Add peeper then stir.

Add the sliced mushrooms.

Sweat out.

De-glaze with brandy& red wine.

Add beef stock reducing by half.

Add the cream.

Bring to boil and simmer.

Chimichurri Sauce

10 Long Red Chillies

2 Bulbs Garlic

1 Bunch Curly Parsley

4 tbsp Oregano

2 tbsp Sea Salt Flakes

200ml Red Wine Vinegar

300ml Extra Virgin Olive Oil

300ml Cold Water

1 Red Onion

De-seed the chillies and finely chop.

Finely chop red onion, parsley and mix together with chillies.

Purée the garlic and add to mix with sea salt.

Add the red wine vinegar, water and oil.

If you haven't chopped the above finely you can always give the mix a quick blitz with a hand blender.

Check the seasoning.

It should not be too sharp or too sweet.

Café de Paris Butter

Ingredients

250g Unsalted Butter

15g Tomato Ketchup

7g Dijon Mustard

7g Capers in Brine

¼ Small Finely Diced Onion

12g Fresh Parsley - Chopped

12g Fresh Chives - Chopped

Pinch Dried Marjoram

Pinch Dried Dill

Pinch Fresh Thyme - Leaves Only

3 Leaves Fresh Tarragon

Dash Ground Rosemary

1 Clove of Garlic - Finely Chopped

2 Anchovy Fillets
- Washed (optional)

1 tsp Brandy

1 tsp Madeira Wine

1 Splash Worcester Sauce

Pinch Sweet Paprika

Pinch Curry Powder

Pinch Cayenne

Pinch Cracked Black Pepper

Juice of ¼ Lemon + Zest

3g Salt

Method

Soften the butter.

All other ingredients should be finely chopped or pulsed in a food processor.

Mix all the items together in a bowl.

In a sheet of silicone paper roll into a log and freeze.

Cut slices as and when needed.

Keeps for several weeks in freezer.

Thai Paste

Ingredients

4 Bulbs Garlic

1 Large (10cm) Piece Ginger

2 Bunches Lemon Grass

10 Chillies

1 Chef Spoon Ground Coriander

1 Chef Spoon Ground Cumin

1 Bunch Fresh Coriander

1 Small Tin Tomato Purée (500g)

6 Lime Leaves

Olive Oil

Seasoning

Method

Split the lemon grass down the middle and finely chop.

Peel the garlic and ginger then roughly chop.

Roughly chop the chillies and fresh coriander.

Place all in a tub with the rest of the ingredients and using a stick blender, blend together until smooth.

Use a small amount of water to get this started then add the olive oil.

Check seasoning. You should be able to taste all the flavours.

Suggestions
This paste can be used to marinate chicken, fish, Halloumi etc.

Make into a sauce.

Use to spice up a soup.

Thai Sauce

4 tbsp Thai Paste

2 Tins Coconut Milk
(400g Tins)

Serving Suggestions
We use 4 strips of Thai paste coated chicken per serving, a cup of cooked rice, and julienne of vegetables, fresh Coriander chopped to garnish.

Julienne vegetables consist of leek, red onions, red, yellow and green peppers all cut very thinly, mixed together and lightly steamed.

Add Thai paste to medium pan and cook out on a small flame.

When this is cooked through add the coconut milk.

Let this cook out together for about 15 - 20 minutes stirring occasionally so it does not stick to the bottom.

Check the seasoning and consistency.

Harissa Paste

Ingredients

3 Large Tomatoes
- Roughly Chopped

2 Red Onions
- Roughly Chopped

3 Large Red Peppers
- Roughly Chopped

3 Chillies
- Roughly Chopped

4 Cloves Garlic
- Peeled

1 Knob of Ginger
- Roughly Chopped

1 Heaped tsp Sweet Paprika

Pinch Cayenne Pepper

Pinch Ground Coriander

1 Tin Tomato Purée

Splash of Olive Oil

Salt and Pepper to Taste

Method

Place all ingredients on tray and roast in oven for about 40 - 60 minutes, until everything is soft.

Blend together until smooth.

Check seasoning.

Desserts

Sticky Toffee Pudding

Ingredients

450g Chopped Dates

Water

1½ tsp Bicarbonate of Soda

150g Butter

450g Caster Sugar

3 Eggs

450g Self Raising Flour

Method

Put dates into a pan with just enough water to cover.

Keep on a low heat and stir.

After 5 minutes add the bicarb.

In a bowl, cream together the butter and sugar.

Add the eggs one at a time then the flour.

Add the cooled dates.

Butter the pudding moulds.

Fill ¾ full and cover individually with foil.

Cook in a bain-marie for 45 minutes - 1 hour on high/full.

Toffee Sauce
250g Soft Dark Brown Sugar

1 Ltr Double Cream

½ Block Unsalted Butter

Sauce Method
Cut up the butter and place in a pan with all the other ingredients.

Simmer and cook through, until the sugar has melted.

Crème Brûlée

Ingredients

200g Caster sugar

12 Egg Yolks

1 Vanilla Pod

1.3 ltr Double Cream

Method

Place cream in pan with vanilla pod and heat up until a skin starts to form.

Whisk the egg yolks and sugar together in a bowl.

Slowly pour the heated cream onto the egg mix whisking continuously.

Pass through a sieve and leave to settle over night.

Pour custard mix into ramekins.

Place in a deep sided tray and pour water around (bain-marie)

Place in oven gas mark 4 (180°C / 160°C fan) for 40mins +/-

Check to see if they are set by shaking them.

They should be set firm and wobble.

Lemon Posset

Ingredients

180cl Double Cream

500g Caster Sugar

6 Lemons
- Juiced

Punnet of Seasonal Berries

50g Caster Sugar

tsp Vanilla Extract

Method

Pour the cream and sugar into a pan and bring to the boil for 2 - 3 minutes.

Add the lemon juice and allow to cool.

Arrange the glasses on a tray.

Pour the cooled liquid into the glasses and chill.

Place in fridge for 2+ hours.

Topping

Slowly warm the berries, sugar and vanilla in a saucepan until the sugar melts.

If they are too dry add a splash of water or appropriate liqueur if you want to give them a boozy kick.

Chocolate Truffle Cake

Ingredients

450g Dark Chocolate Buttons

570ml Double Cream

4 Egg Yolks

200g Caster Sugar

Chocolate Genoese Sponge

Ganache Topping for Truffle Cake
400g Dark Chocolate Buttons

50ml Double Cream

28g Unsalted Butter
- cut small

Ganache Preparation
Melt the chocolate butter and cream gently together over a bain-marie.

Once the mousse is set pour ganache over and return to fridge to set.

Portion to required sizes.

Method

Line a deep sided tray with silicone paper.

Place a thin layer of chocolate sponge in the tray.

Some alcohol can be added at this stage if required - do not soak.

Place the chocolate and half of the cream in a bowl, over a pan of water (bain-marie) until melted then take off pan to cool slightly.

Semi whip the other half of the cream in a bowl.

In a separate bowl whisk the egg yolks and sugar together until pale and fluffy.

Add the egg mix to the heated chocolate mix. (This will ensure the eggs are cooked)

Mix well.

Now fold in the semi whipped cream ensuring it is mixed well.

Now pour this mix on to the sponge in the lined tray.

Chill in the fridge.

Once set pour on the Ganache

Panettone
Bread & Butter Pudding

Ingredients

1 Large Panettone

1 Block of Unsalted Butter

5 Eggs

370ml Double Cream

200ml Milk

70g Sugar

1 Vanilla Pod

Sultanas

Marmalade

Cinnamon

Method

Mix the eggs and sugar together in a bowl.

Bring milk, cream and vanilla to the boil.

Pour over eggs and mix.

Strain through a sieve.

Butter line a deep sided tray.

Place a layer of buttered Panettone, sprinkle of sultanas, pinch of cinnamon and a spread of marmalade.

Layer until tray is almost full.

Pour over the custard mix.

Press down on the bread and leave to absorb the mix.

Cover with foil.

Place in oven on a low heat and cook Gas mark 1 - 2 (150°C / 130°C fan) for 40 mins - 1 hour

Should be moist when set.

Crème Anglaise
& Custard

Ingredients

Crème Anglaise
450ml Milk

8 Egg Yolks

115g Caster Sugar

2 Vanilla Pods

Custard
2 tbsp Cornflour

Method

Crème Anglaise
Whisk egg yolks and sugar together until pale.

Add vanilla pods to milk and bring to a near boil forming a skin.

Pour milk over eggs then pour back into pan.

Cook out gently.

DO NOT ALLOW TO BOIL.

Should thicken slightly and coat the back of a spoon.

Strain through sieve.

Custard Method
As above

Add the cornflour to the egg and sugar.

Pour the milk then add back to the pan

Cook out, stirring continuously until thick.

Strain through sieve.

Cocktails

Cocktails - a Brief History...

The word "cocktail" first appeared in print in 1806

The golden age of cocktails was between 1860 and 1920. However, it was the roaring "twenties" that saw cocktails come into their own. Unfortunately this also coincided with a very unhappy state of affairs in the USA called Prohibition (1920 - 1933).

This era forced drinkers underground into illicit bars known as "speakeasies". These bars weren't dives, but luxuriously decorated bars and more importantly female friendly which brought added glamour to the cocktail. Because liquor was illegal, bootleg or moonshine was drunk instead but this was often so vile that bartenders would mix it with juices and cordials to mask its aggressive taste.

Bartenders who did not wish to break the law went to Europe and Cuba to ply their trade. Many of the cocktails we count as classics today, from the Bloody Mary to the Mojito, were invented overseas during this time.

Prohibition ended in 1933 shortly after President Franklin D. Roosevelt came into office. An accomplished drinker and handy bartender himself, FDR along with Winston Churchill was a great advocate of the cocktail, especially the Martini. Indeed, it was during a summit meeting between Stalin, Churchill and Roosevelt in 1943 that Roosevelt himself first whipped up Dirty Martinis for the powerful trio.

Women were welcomed with open arms into the cocktail lounges of the 1930s. Although there were still laws in some American states prohibiting them from ordering drinks at the bar, this was easily solved by the introduction of table service and with it, glamour and style to cocktail drinking.

The 60s was something of a none starter when it came to cocktails. Free love and the drug culture made the cocktail look stuffy, but It was the 1990s that saved the scene. People now wanted quality cocktails made from premium spirits and exotic fruits and juices. Bartenders started looking more and more to the kitchen for new ingredients, and so it was, the mixologist was truly born.

Revised article by Marc Vermiglio
Restaurant Manager and Cocktail Lush

Tips for Tastier Tipples

Some of our favourite cocktails are quite easy to make at home.
If you follow some simple rules you'll be able to make beautiful drinks that taste as good as if prepared by the pros.

Rule 1 - Ingredients are key

- Try to use the freshest fruits and herbs you can find.

- Cheap spirits will make for a cheap tasting drink. Leave that cut-price booze well alone!

- Always use fresh, clean ice. Old ice stored in your freezer at home can collect odours and flavours from food.

- Never re-use ice from a cocktail shaker in your drinks. Fresh ice keeps your drinks colder for longer and prevents excess dilution.

- Wash & Roll citrus fruits – if you are using citrus fruit, a great way to get more juice from it is to soak the fruit in warm water - this softens the fruit and removes any wax from the skin.
  Rolling the fruit on a hard surface with the palm of your hand works really well to soften the fruit and releases more flavoursome oils from the zesty skin.

Rule 2 - Find the Balance

- A balanced drink should be not too sweet and not too sour - aim for the middle. If it's too sweet add more citrus, if it's too sour add more sugar.

- Harmony - just like a great piece of music, a cocktail's ingredients should be in perfect harmony and compliment one another.

- Accuracy and measuring are always important. The slightest adjustment to a recipe can change a drink hugely. Getting the proportions just right is what makes a good drink amazing!

Rule 3 - Keep it simple

- Remember you don't need 17 ingredients when 3 or 4 will do. You should be able to taste each component – they should be there for a reason!

- Stronger does not mean better. Adding more alcohol to a drink doesn't make it a better drink.

- Try experimenting with bitters. They are great for adding an intense hit of flavour to a drink in just a few drops.

DIY - You may have all the equipment you need at home

- A jam jar can make a pretty good cocktail shaker

- A humble tea strainer works well as a cocktail fine strainer.

- Egg cups make great spirit measures.

- To make your own crushed ice at home simply wrap cubed ice in a clean tea towel, scrunch up the corners so none can escape and bash with a rolling pin.

- A rolling pin makes a good muddler for mashing ingredients too.

- Sugar syrup is an important ingredient in many cocktails. To make your own simply boil some fresh water in a pan and add white sugar and stir until the granules have all melted. Use 2 parts sugar to 1 part water for the best dilution.

Berry Collins

Ingredients

25ml Good Quality Gin

25ml Chambord

½ Lemon

5 Mashed Fresh Strawberries

Dash Sugar Syrup

Shake well and strain into a tall glass.

Top with soda.

Garnish with a ½ strawberry.

Bloody Mary

Ingredients

50ml Good Quality Vodka

4 Dashes Worcestershire Sauce

2 Small drops of Tabasco Sauce

Add more for an extra spicy kick

1 Squeezed Lemon Wedge

1 Squeezed Lime Wedge

3 Grinds Black Pepper

175ml Good Quality Tomato Juice

Stir ingredients over ice and strain into a tall glass with 2 fresh ice cubes.

Garnish with a celery stick and a slice of lemon.

There are many stories about the origins of the Bloody Mary. One such legend has it that the drink was first served to Hemingway in Paris. As the story goes, his doctors had forbidden him from having alcohol and his wife, Mary, was holding him to it. A bartender at the Ritz mixed him the vodka-&-tomato juice drink, full of booze that could not be detected thanks to the other strong ingredients. Having got the better of his "bloody wife," the cocktail was christened after her.

Caipirinha

Ingredients

50ml Cachaça White Spirit

1 Diced Lime

2 bar spoons of White Sugar

Build in rocks glass, muddle lime, sugar and spirit, top with crushed ice, stir, add more crushed ice.

Cachaça, a spirit indigenous to Brazil, is distilled directly from the juice of sugar cane. The Caipirinha means "little peasant girl". It is one of the great classic cocktails of the world and the national drink of Brazil. With its principal ingredient – Cachaça – the drink is protected by law as the national patrimony of Brazil.

Cosmopolitan

Ingredients

37.5ml Vodka

12.5ml Cointreau

50ml Cranberry Juice

2 Squeezed Lime Wedges

Shake all ingredients and strain into a chilled Martini glass.

Garnish with a strip of orange zest - spray the zesty oil over the drink first.

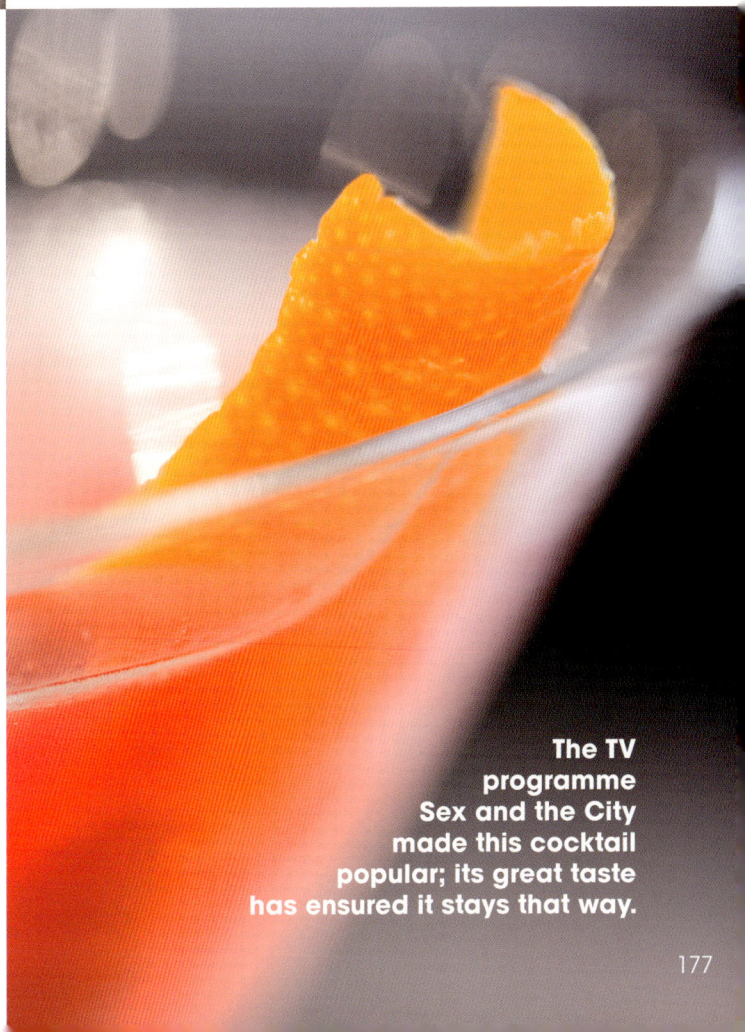

The TV programme Sex and the City made this cocktail popular; its great taste has ensured it stays that way.

Berry Bellini

Ingredients

12.5ml Vodka

12.5ml Chambord Black Raspberry Liqueur

3 Mashed Fresh Strawberries

- Any Seasonal Berry Will Work

Small Dash of Sugar Syrup

Shake ingredients and strain into a Champagne flute.

Top with Prosecco and gently stir.

Garnish with ½ a strawberry.

Elderflower Mojito

Ingredients

25ml Havana Club 3 Year Rum

25ml St. Germain Elderflower Liqueur

8 – 12 Mint Leaves

½ a Diced Lime

1 Tea Spoon of White Sugar

Build in a tall glass, muddle lime, sugar and spirit, add mint, muddle lightly again, top with crushed ice, stir, add a splash of soda and top with crushed ice.

Garnish with a mint sprig.

For a classic Mojito just ditch the St Germain and replace with an extra shot of Havana and an extra spoon of sugar.

Havana is the birthplace of the Mojito. Some historians contend that African slaves who worked in the Cuban sugar cane fields during the 19th century were instrumental in the cocktail's origin. The sugar cane juice often used in Mojitos, was a popular drink amongst the slaves who helped coin the name of the sweet nectar.

Espresso Martini

Ingredients

37.5ml Vodka

12.5ml Kahlua Coffee Liqueur

1 Strong Espresso

Dash of Gomme

All ingredients in shaker -

shake hard and fast.

Double strain into chilled Martini glass.

Garnish with 3 coffee beans.

With its dark velvety body and creamy top, the espresso Martini was designed both to wake up and to calm down simultaneously.

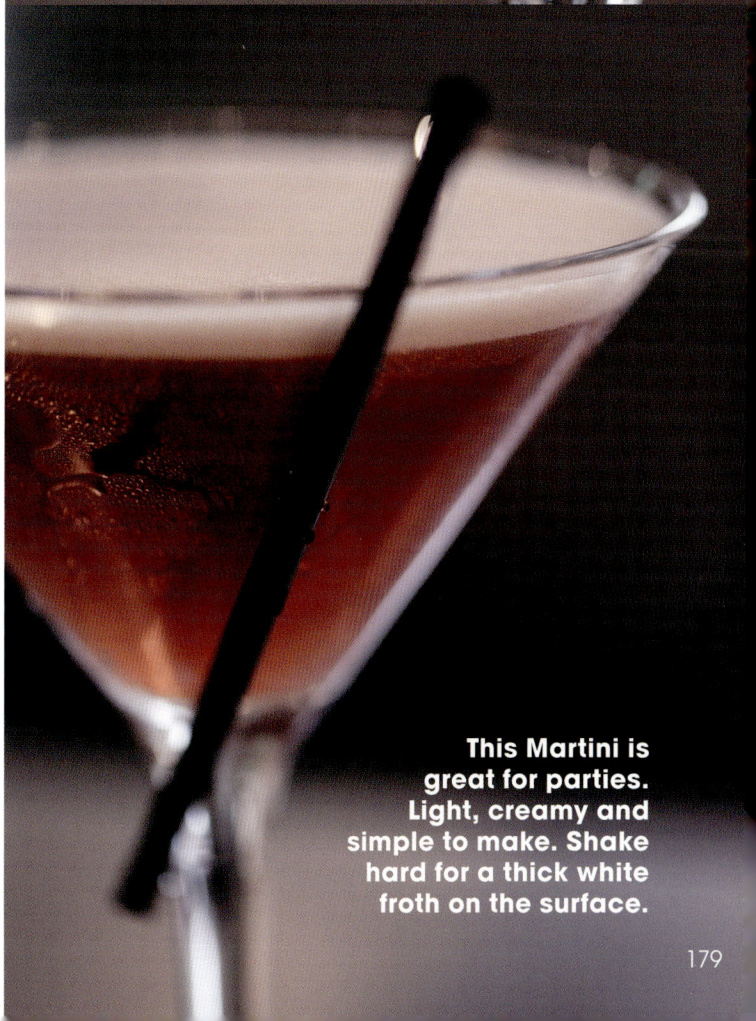

French Martini

Ingredients

37.5ml Absolut Vodka

12.5ml Chambord

50ml Pineapple Juice

Shake all ingredients really hard and strain into a chilled Martini glass.

This Martini is great for parties. Light, creamy and simple to make. Shake hard for a thick white froth on the surface.

Mango Mai Tai

Ingredients

25ml Good Quality Aged Rum

12.5ml Dark Rum

12.5ml Cointreau

Dash of Almond (Orgeat) Syrup

Dash of Sugar Syrup

50ml of Fresh Mango Juice

2 Squeezed Limes

Shake all ingredients and strain into a tall glass or a large tumbler over crushed ice.

Garnish with a mint sprig and orange peel.

Margarita

Ingredients

37.5ml Good Aged Tequila

12.5ml Cointreau

6 Lime Wedges Squeezed and Dropped in

2 Squeezed Lemon Wedges

Dash of Sugar Syrup

Shake ingredients and strain into a chilled Martini glass with a salt rim.

- To salt the rim wipe lime juice around the rim, hold the glass by the stem pointing towards the floor and sprinkle salt over the glass.

Garnish with lime peel or a lime wedge.

One of the earliest stories is of the Margarita being invented in 1938 by Carlos "Danny" Herrera at his restaurant in Mexico, created for customer and former Ziegfeld dancer Marjorie King, who was allergic to many spirits, but not to Tequila.

Whisky Sour

Ingredients

50ml Scotch Whisky
Juice of ½ a Lemon with a couple of
wedges dropped into shaker
20ml Sugar Syrup
1 Egg White

Shake all ingredients really well and strain
into a rocks glass over cubed ice.

Garnish with a lemon and a cherry.

Old Fashioned

Ingredients

50ml good quality Bourbon
- or try it with aged Rum or Tequila
1 heaped teaspoon of brown sugar
Dash of Angostura bitters

Place a dash of the spirit, the sugar
and bitters into a rocks glass with 1 ice
cube and stir slowly as the ice melts.

Add another dash of spirit and 1 more
ice cube and keep stirring.

Repeat until all the sugar has dissolved
and stir in a strip of orange zest.

The Bell

Anyone who has dined at The Lead Station will have heard the ringing of our bell.

Demanding respect and prompt attention, it rules over 99 Beech Road. The subtleties of its chimes are their own code - speaking volumes and informing its subjects of the reception they might receive when answering its' call.

From "food to go" to the thunderous ring of "Get this food out – Now!" it is not to be messed with, taken lightly or dismissed – ever!

If ever a bell could forewarn of Chef's mood, then this bell delivers its' message clearly. An awkward check can leave quivering servers waiting for the bell, summoning them to explain themselves to Chef.

For 20 years this bell has terrified staff, bemused customers and given the power of a dictator to our kitchen. It has encouraged our young bussers to grow thicker skins, learn some defensive arts and grow in character. It has inspired staff to engage in diplomacy whilst also increase their speed of movement dramatically.

It has though, most importantly, maintained order in the restaurant, tolling whenever it is time to serve.

If The Lead Station were an orchestra, Joanie would be just left of the conductor on first desk. The bell plays her tune and long may it ring out.

Conversion Table

METRIC	IMPERIAL
10g	1/4oz
15g	1/2oz
30g	1oz
60g	2oz
90g	3oz
125g	4oz (1/4 lb)
155g	5oz
185g	6oz
220g	7oz
250g	8oz (1/2lb)
280g	9oz
315g	10oz
345g	11oz
375g	12oz (3/4 lb)
410g	13oz
440g	14oz
470g	15oz
500g (1/2kg)	16oz (1 lb)
750g	24oz (1 1/2lb)
1kg	32oz (2 lb)
1.5kg	48oz (3 lb)

METRIC	IMPERIAL
30ml	1 fl oz
60ml	2 fl oz
80ml	3 1/2 fl oz
100ml	2 3/4 fl oz
125ml	4 fl oz
150ml	5 fl oz
180ml	6 fl oz
200ml	7 fl oz
250ml	8 3/4 fl oz
310ml	10 1/2 fl oz
375ml	13 fl oz
430ml	15 fl oz
475ml	16 fl oz
500ml	17 fl oz
625ml	21 1/2 fl oz
750ml	26 fl oz
1L	35 fl oz
1.25L	44 fl oz
1.5L	52 fl oz
2L	70 fl oz
2.5L	80 fl oz

°C electric	°C fan	°F	GAS
120°	100°	250°	1
150°	130°	300°	2
160°	140°	325°	3
180°	160°	350°	4
190°	170°	375°	5
200°	180°	400°	6
230°	210°	450°	7
250°	230°	500°	9